FAMOUS AIRCRAFT OF THE NATIONAL AIR AND SPACE MUSEUM

VOLUME 1
EXCALIBUR III
The Story of a P-51 Mustang

VOLUME 2
THE AERONCA C-2
The Story of the Flying Bathtub

VOLUME 3
THE P-80 SHOOTING STAR
Evolution of a Jet Fighter

VOLUME 4
ALBATROS D. Va
German Fighter of World War I

VOLUME 5
BLERIOT XI
The Story of a Classic Aircraft

VOLUME 6
BELLANCA C.F.
The Emergence of the Cabin Monoplane
in the United States

VOLUME 7
de Havilland DH-4
From Flaming Coffin to Living Legend

de Havilland DH-4

From
Flaming Coffin
to
Living Legend

by Walter J. Boyne

PUBLISHED FOR THE

National Air and Space Museum

BY THE

Smithsonian Institution Press

WASHINGTON, D.C.
1984

Cover art by John F. Amendola, Jr.

Frontispiece:
The Dayton-Wright FS—the first attempt of the company to design an airplane. FS stood for "first shot," which was Dayton, Ohio, vernacular for "initial attempt." Howard Rinehart, redoubtable Dayton-Wright test pilot, is in the cockpit.

Unless otherwise indicated, all photographs are from the files of the National Air and Space Museum

Library of Congress Cataloging in Publication Data

Boyne, Walter J., 1929-
   De Havilland DH-4.

   Bibliography: p.
   1. DH-4 bomber.   I. Title.
UG1242.B6B686   1984   358.4'2   84-1391
ISBN 0-87474-277-3 (pbk.)

The paper in this book meets the guidelines for permanence and durability of the Committee on Production Guidelines for Book Longevity of the Council on Library Resources.

Contents

Foreword

Maligned by the public and the news media, viewed with mixed emotions by the men who serviced and flew it, the de Havilland DH-4 emerged as the only American-produced aircraft to see combat service during World War I, and endured for years thereafter because of a fortuitous combination of circumstances and good basic design.

Walter J. Boyne has told the history of this wonderful airplane with characteristic candor, attention to detail, and the imaginative use of personal vignettes that blend the human element with the necessary technical details. The DH-4 was based on a design by the brilliant British engineer, Geoffrey de Havilland, and was the very fortunate result of extraordinary measures taken by the U.S. government and industry as the U.S. entered the war in Europe. Proper funding, organization, and industrial mobilization eventually led to production of over 4,800 DH-4s in the United States, most of which were built by the Dayton-Wright Airplane Company.

As a warplane, the DH-4 performed its combat role as bomber and observation plane in excellent fashion. Despite operational problems due to design deficiencies and production defects, the DH-4 gradually came into its own, and by the end of the war in 1918, American pilots and their DH-4s had become a proficient fighting team. Its abbreviated combat tour merely set the stage for the DH-4's illustrious postwar service in both military and civilian roles. Surplus DH-4s appeared in films, patrolled for forest fires, and flew the mail. The airplane continued to perform numerous functions for the Army and Navy, many of which are highlighted by Boyne through the use of personal recollections by such famous figures as Jimmy Doolittle, Leigh Wade, and Lawrence Craigie. The remembrances of these renowned airmen and generals add substance and humor to the account of the decade of the 1920s.

The story of the restoration of the National Air and Space Museum's DH-4, Dayton-Wright's No. 1 prototype, is told by the skilled craftsmen who actually performed the work. The narration is technical, but understandable, and also thoroughly entertaining, and should have considerable appeal to amateur and professional craftsmen alike.

Appendices compare the DH-4's performance to that of other well-known World War I aircraft, and the airplane holds up quite well with its competition in many respects. The performance summaries and other technical data in the appendices are fitting conclusions to this seventh volume in the Famous Aircraft of the National Air and Space Museum series.

E.T. WOOLDRIDGE

Chairman

Aeronautics Department

National Air and Space Museum

Acknowledgments

Many people and many sources helped me with this book, and I am grateful to the scholars and authors who wrote on the subject before me, as well as to those who so willingly assisted in reading, commenting, and proofing.

A number of persons have done excellent work on the history of both the English de Havilland D.H.4 and the American-built de Havilland DH-4, including the redoubtable Jack Bruce, former Keeper of the Royal Air Force Museum at Hendon, and formerly the Lindbergh Professor of the National Air and Space Museum; Peter M. Bowers, a legend in his own time in the field of aviation history, home builts, aircraft markings, models, and so on; and Robert Casari, who has done an excellent job in investigating the American World War I production effort.

In addition, I had excellent assistance from Chairman Tim Wooldridge, Jay Spenser, Claudia Oakes, Bob van der Linden, and Bob Mikesh, all of the National Air and Space Museum Aeronautics Department, as well as the always welcome guiding hand of Don Lopez, the Museum's Deputy Director. These stalwart souls read my manuscript over and over, and made many suggestions that I incorporated.

In a similar way I received outstanding help from outside reviewers. Bob Cavanagh did his customary meticulous job, adding much insight into the relative advantages and disadvantages of the DH-4. Peter M. Grosz, our first Verville Fellow, offered many constructive suggestions. Robert Casari, who has published so much on the subject, and has had an especial affection for the DH-4, did a very exacting job of analysis in making his review, and provided me with much excellent material.

I also received help here at the Museum from Larry Wilson, Karl Schneide, Pete Suthard, Dana Bell, Nancy Shaw, Helen McMahon, Ed Pupek, Frank Pietropaoli, and the always enthusiastic Phil Edwards. Alice Adams and Janis Davidson worked the word processer for me with the assistance of Efrain Ortiz and Vicki Rosenberg.

Peter Bowers supplied a wonderful set of photos, as did the Air Force Museum, where Vivian White performed her usual miracles. Dale Hrabak did an excellent job of photography, as he always does.

The restoration effort was conducted under the general guidance of Bob Mikesh's curatorial package, Walter Roderick's supervision, using the talents of Rich Horigan and Karl Heinzel. Also assisting were Wil Powell, Joe Fichera, Jim Cusack, and others.

First hand accounts of flying the aircraft came from Major General Leigh Wade, USAF (Retired), Lt. General Laurence Craigie, USAF (Retired), and artist Guy Wiser Brown, who was shot down in a DH-4 over German territory. Brigadier General Harold R. Harris, USAF (Retired) also supplied some colorful anecdotes on the airplane.

John Amendola did his usual first rate work on the cover painting, capturing not only the prototype DH-4, but also the flavor of the Dayton-Wright era. In Dayton, I received assistance from the Hall of Fame, from the Montgomery County Historical Society, and from Darlene Gerhardt, the indefatigable chronicler of the McCook Field period.

A special word of praise should go to Felix Lowe, Director of the Smithsonian Institution Press, who has done so much for the Institution's publications program.

To everyone, and especially to those whom I have inevitably but unfortunately forgotten to acknowledge, my thanks.

de Havilland DH-4

Introduction

The reputations of aircraft, like those of men, often hang more on a well-turned phrase than on a lifetime of endeavor. The de Havilland DH-4[1] lives on in public memory as a "flaming coffin,"[2] the product of the wasteful aviation effort of World War I, a sort of accident-prone albatross, a death ship, a crate that you can't send boys up in. This reputation is terribly unfair.

The DH-4, or Liberty Plane as it was called at a time when sauerkraut was "Liberty Cabbage" and dachshunds were "Liberty Dogs," was perhaps the most used, as well as the most maligned, U.S. aircraft of World War I. Despite all argument to the contrary, it had one outstanding virtue that transcended all faults and that made it the single most important aircraft in U.S. Army service until the late 1920s. That virtue was availability, for the DH-4, for a variety of reasons, was built in greater numbers than any other combat plane manufactured in the United States and as a result dominated the postwar service simply by always being there.[3]

The de Havilland was not a perfect airplane—far from it; yet it had performance that was sensational when introduced by the English in 1917, was still adequate when the war ended, and was the only U.S.-manufactured aircraft to engage in combat. There were inherent problems in the design that were reluctantly accepted to keep the production rate high. The original location of the fuselage fuel tank was unfortunate in that it not only hampered crew coordination, but also was a lethal hazard to the pilot in the event of a crash because of its location and inadequate structure. The landing gear was placed too far aft, and there were many nose-overs. The construction of the fuselage with its long wooden longerons and wire bracing, while perfectly normal for the time, resulted in crash fatalities due to splintering and impalement that could have been avoided by a stronger steel tube structure.

On the positive side, the DH-4 was a reliable aircraft with good speed and load capability. With its high aspect ratio wings and large tail perched at the end of a long fuselage, it was stable in flight and relatively pleasant to fly. Lack of adequate trimming devices—common at the time—made it tiring to fly over long distances.

Lost in all consideration of the aircraft has been the fact that it was designed only 13 years after the Wright brothers' first flight and, while it was not significantly different from its contemporaries, it was not equalled in all-around performance by any German observation aircraft.[4]

Part of this performance was, of course, due to the superb engines that powered it; the British primarily used a Rolls Royce Eagle of 275 horsepower, a classic engine often in short supply because of the demands made upon it by other aircraft types, while the Americans used, naturally enough, their famous Liberty engine, a design accomplishment and production miracle.

In appearance, the DH-4 was conventional. It was a two-bay biplane of 42 feet, 6 inch span; the fuselage, somewhat spindly in appearance, was about thirty feet long. With a gross weight of approximately 4,300 pounds, the American DH-4 was armed with two Lewis guns mounted on a Scarff ring in the rear cockpit and one or two forward-firing Marlin machine guns, a formidable combination for the time. It could haul 322 pounds of bombs over a range of 100 miles and could be equipped, as the mission demanded, with cameras or for wireless telegraphy.

We'll examine some contemporary aircraft for comparison purposes later, but it is sufficient to say here that the top speed of the clean, lightly loaded

DH-4, 124 mph, was faster than most German fighters of the time, right up to the closing days of the war.

DH-4* Liberty 400 HP	Fokker** D VII F BMW IIIa/185HP	Fokker** D VIII	Junkers** J9/DI	Roland D VI b
124.7 mph @ sea level	124.3 mph @ sea level	126.8 mph @ sea level	149 mph @ sea level	124.3 mph @ sea level
117 mph/10000'	127.4 mph @			
113 mph/15000'	6562'			

*J.M. Bruce, 1957, p. 179.
**Kroschel & Stutzer, 1977, p. 147.

Heavily loaded, the DH-4 was of course, much slower, and was unable to climb as high as desired.

The period of time in which the American DH-4 was selected for production, procured, produced, and sent to the front was incredibly compressed: the U.S. entered the war on April 6, 1917; the DH-4 was selected for production in July 1917; the first aircraft rolled out of the factory on October 29, 1917; and the first appeared in France on May 11, 1918. The first flight over enemy lines took place on August 9, and when the war ended there were 196 American-built DH-4s in twelve units at the front.

But this service was perhaps the least of the DH-4's accomplishments for, in truth, the U.S. Air Service was just learning how to fight when the war ended. During the postwar period, when most Air Service aircraft were either war-surplus, or re-manufactured DH-4s, it was the most versatile aircraft in the United States. It flew the mail, dusted crops, raced, and served as the workhorse in numerous experiments. More important than all of these, though, was the fact that it was a combat aircraft, however obsolete, in which pilots, mechanics and observers could practice their trade. It became more demanding of piloting and mechanical skills as it grew older, and required a degree of resourcefulness on the part of its units to maintain an operational readiness that served as excellent training for the war years ahead. The degree of influence of the aircraft may be estimated by the fact that during the 21-year interval between the wars, the DH-4 was in extensive use for more than half the period.

Despite all of its accomplishments and the enormous burden borne by its long but slender wings over the decade of the 1920s, the pejorative "flaming coffin" name was never entirely forgotten. The DH-4's reputation would not have been so roundly besmirched had it not been for the coincidental furor over the alleged misuse of the massive $640,000,000 appropriation that Congress had made for aviation in the first days of World War I. Perhaps guilt-ridden by the shameless neglect of aviation in the years from 1903 to 1917, the Congress had overreacted by pledging more in this appropriation than had ever been done for a single purpose before. In doing so, it raised the expectations of press and public for a cloud of aircraft to issue from American factories exactly as Model Ts issued from the Ford plants. Yankee pride and ingenuity could be expected to solve this little matter of the combat airplane overnight—the airplane had, after all, been invented in America and, once the production geniuses in Detroit had studied the problem a bit, there would be a true darkening of the skies over Europe with American battleplanes. (There might possibly be an analogy in this to the massive catch-up efforts of the Kennedy missile gap and the current Reagan rearming program.)

The fact that no basis for an American aircraft industry had existed prior to mid-year 1917 was irrelevant to the Congress, the public, and the press; and no amount of subsequent explanation could ever put it in perspective. Before the war ended, prematurely from the point of view of the fruition of the American aviation industry, there were journalistic and Congressional allegations of fraud, mismanagement, collusion, sabotage, and worse.

There were probably some elements of truth in all of these charges—it was still a free enterprise system and a $640,000,000 "golden goose" wasn't going to go unplucked by the unscrupulous. But in the main the leaders, by stress, strain, genius, and luck, set up in a year's time the foundation for what would have been the most massive, modern air force in the world. Almost overnight, substantial industries were created, and these depended upon a network of sub-contractors, farmers, lumbermen, and transportation experts that extended across the forty-eight states. New products, new methods, new standards and new concepts of scale had all been successfully introduced. New models of combat-quality aircraft were not only being designed, but were getting set for mass production. And in the midst of all of this, no less than 3,431 DH-4s were turned out, with 1,213 being delivered overseas by the end of the war. When production was finally terminated in March 1919, a total of 4,846 had been built in U.S. factories.

Let's see how it began and how it ended.

Dayton-Wright, unlike many of the other war-time manufacturers who operated out of hanger-like barns, set up a complete modern manufacturing system, designed with an eye for post-war production possibilities. Plant No. 1 had been built to manufacture DELCO lighting equipment for farmers; its size, shape and location made it admirably suited for the production of aircraft. It is still in existence. (See also next page.)

The Primitive Beginnings

It is almost impossible to understand today why the United States, which had given birth to the airplane and which has exercised a proprietary smugness about it for the last fifty years, was so absolutely indifferent to its development during the crucial 1903-1914 period. It is even harder to understand, in view of the rapture with which Europe embraced all aspects of flight, and in view of the finances, engineering, and manpower it invested.

Part of it has to do with the crass Yankee commercialism of the period. It was obvious that there was no way to make money with an airplane commercially; a few could be sold for sporting or exhibition purposes, but freight or passenger traffic was not profitable. (The remarkable American highway and rail systems would keep the airplane from being competitive for another thirty years.) On the other hand the American military establishment was so poverty stricken that it could not in good conscience risk a great deal of money on a new, controversial, and as yet unproven device. The production of the de Havilland DH-4 by the U.S. may be said to have occurred despite, rather than because of, the funding. Fortunately, the dedicated personnel and the almost haphazard organizational set-up of U.S. governmental agencies somehow combined to make the American DH-4 possible.

Funding
Aviation in America sputtered along, virtually fixed at the limited capability of the early Wright and Curtiss types, because the general level of government investment was so low. From 1908 to 1913 Germany had spent over $28,000,000 on aviation, France had spent $22,000,000, Russia $12,000,000, and even Brazil $500,000. The United States had spent only $435,000. In the year immediately before the outbreak of the war Germany spent a staggering $45,000,000; France almost $13,000,000; Russia, considering her impoverished state, an astonishing $22,500,000; and the United States $250,000

Perhaps more amazingly, even after the hard evidence of 1914, 1915, and 1916, when aerial warfare in all its modern forms had been demonstrated, and when the United States itself had had first-hand experience with aviation in the Mexican Expedition, there was no significant swell of opinion—civil or military—for even a modest increase in aviation expenditure.

For the first eight years beginning with 1908, 59 aircraft had been ordered and 54 delivered from four different companies to the United States Army. By late 1916, after the long exchange of bellicose notes between the U.S. and Germany, only 366 planes had been ordered and only a small percentage of these delivered. In 1917, American observers had witnessed Bloody April in which the German Air Force had almost destroyed the British Royal Flying Corps, yet they were unable to translate their genuine concern into more than token action on the part of either the Army or the Congress.

Then, after this long dry spell, money began to flow, creeping through Congressional resistance like water through a crack in a dam. An unprecedented $13,281,666 was authorized in August 1916, and this was supple-

mented in May 1917, just a month after America had entered the war, by another $10,800,000. These amounts were staggering for the time and were almost an embarrassment in that there was virtually no industry from which to procure the needed aircraft and supplies. Despite a lack of capital, the Curtiss Aeroplane Company was in a period of vigorous growth and had contracts to supply JN-4s and flying boats to the Allies, but there was no other manufacturer worth noting. As eager designers and promoters sprang to fill the gap and create aircraft and production sites, it soon became apparent that there was no industrial substructure to supply the required materials and components; there were insufficent quantities of spruce, linen, dope, instruments, etc. Most critical of all, there was no engine manufacturer producing a combat quality engine.

Personnel

The lack of funds and career promise did not make the Aeronautical Division of the Signal Corps attractive to most bright young officers. The very real prospect of injury and the remote location of flying fields were additional drawbacks.

Fortunately, a few brave and visionary officers were willing to accept the risk necessary to shape the infant service into an organization that could be expanded when war came. They took their lead from Lt. Colonel George O. Squier, one of those extremely rare Army officers who combine genuine scientific skill with an appreciation for the future. An 1887 graduate of West Point, Squier, in 1896, demonstrated his scientific acumen with an invention that greatly improved the ability of land telegraph wires to carry messages. His talents immediately were required by the Signal Corps, which he joined upon the outbreak of war with Spain. In 1899, he created a dynamo that sent an unbroken alternating current over cable, permitting uninterrupted service and doubling its use. He obtained a Ph.D. from Johns Hopkins University in 1903, and at 38 was surely one of the best qualified and most brilliant officers in the Army.

Squier was selected to prepare the specifications for the first military aircraft based on his study of the subject, and he flew as a passenger in a Wright airplane in 1908.

In what was undoubtedly a mixed blessing, Squire served from 1912 to 1916 as a military attache in Great Britain. On the one hand he was divorced from American aeronautics, and it is possible that he might have been able to secure greater appropriations if he had been in the United States during these years to guide the development of the service. On the other hand, in London he was able to keep fully informed on the rapid development of the air weapon at the front.

This experience was of great advantage to him when he was recalled to the United States to take charge of the Aviation Section of the Army in June 1916. With his combined communication/flying background he was a natural choice and, in February 1917, he was appointed Chief Signal Officer with a rank of Brigadier General.

Dayton-Wright was blessed with an abundance of engineering, managerial and production talent. Not many firms of the time had Orville Wright on their engineering staff, a "Boss" Kettering as president, and members of the Talbott family for financial backing.

The Dayton-Wright firm was very modern; new building, new equipment, new methods. These machine tools would not look out of place in a modern factory, except for the overhead belt drive.

A typical scene, with all the workers "frozen" for as long as it took to get the exposure. Normally in photos like this there are blurs where people moved before the picture was finished. Good shop discipline here.

American women went to war in far greater numbers (proportionately in the aero industry) in the first war than German women did in the second. One old joke of the period was that people in the states south of Ohio learned the three Rs in school— "reading, righting and the road to Dayton." The women here are making wire assemblies for bracing.

Typical of the resourcefulness of the time was the fact that production went on as the extension of the factory went up. Note workers on rudder of DH-4 at right. It was a "can do" time.

Preliminary Organization

When the United States entered the war on April 6, 1917, the Aeronautics Division of the Signal Corps comprised 131 officers and 1,087 enlisted men. There were a total of seven undermanned squadrons, strung out between San Antonio and the Philippines. Of the 55 trainer planes available, 51 were considered obsolete. There were no combat aircraft at all and no factories in the country capable of immediately designing or producing one. But there was one thing in abundance—advice.

The fact that U.S. aviation survived the torrent of advice unleashed upon it is a tribute to the motivation and good will of the advisors. The need to somehow create an instant Air Service to meet both the needs of the war and the dreams of its champions called forth a series of ad hoc decisions that spawned an intricate, interrelated series of boards and councils, which must be treated chronologically to make any sense at all.

Fortunately for the war effort, a small group of far-seeing men had done some vital preliminary work in 1915 to set up the National Advisory Committee for Aeronautics (NACA). In some respects almost a Smithsonian cabal, the group had as its prime movers Charles D. Walcott and Alexander Graham Bell, who provided the guidance and the prestige to enhance the basic work of Jerome Hunsaker and Washington Chambers. A group of congressman, led by Henry Cabot Lodge, skillfully attached a rider to the Naval Appropriation Act of March 3, 1915, which established NACA to supervise and direct the scientific study of flight. Only $5,000 per year for five years was allocated, but it was the small essential start of what eventually became the National Aeronautics and Space Administration (NASA) and led eventually to journeys to the moon and beyond.

Almost the first task essayed by the Committee was a survey sent to academic and industrial institutions asking what they were doing in aviation. There were almost no replies that indicated any interest in or, perhaps more importantly, any funding for aviation. Only two universities, the Massachusetts Institute of Technology and the University of Michigan, had regular courses of instruction in aviation.

In time, however, NACA became more concerned with the manifold

Modern psychological methods were not neglected, as this production chart indicates.

problems of production; for the Air Service, despite the upward trend of appropriations, was so small that it was swamped with the problems of training. Until the National Defense Act of June 3, 1916, the Aviation Section had been limited by law to 60 officers and 260 men. The relative lack of appeal of a career in the Aviation Section tended to keep it understaffed and resulted in its being manned largely by younger officers who did not have the experience to address the opportunities for expansion.

As a part of this process Congress established the Council for National Defense on August 29, 1916, and this in its turn set up the Aircraft Production Board on May 16, 1917, a little over one month after the U.S. entered World War I.

The Aircraft Production Board (APB) was intended to facilitate production by coordinating the Army and Navy's selection of aircraft. Like NACA, the Aircraft Production Board was not in the military chain of command and could reach operating personnel in the Army or Navy only by going through Cabinet-level officials.

The APB was chaired by Howard Coffin, who brought his automotive experience with the Hudson Motor Car Company to bear on the proceedings. Coffin knew that standardization was the *sine qua non* of production and, to achieve this, a Joint Army-Navy Technical Board was formed in May, 1917 as a result of an agreement among the Secretary of War (Newton D. Baker), the Secretary of the Navy (Josephus Daniels) and the Chairman of NACA (C. D. Walcott).

The Joint Army-Navy Technical Board was intended to ensure not only that the best aircraft were selected but that there was the maximum possible coordination between the two services.

At this point, no one had yet defined what the size or composition of either the army or navy air forces would be. Then came a clarion call from France, a message so opportune in timing and so stirring in content that it became the basis for the production program. Premier Alexander F. Ribot of France cabled President Wilson on May 26, 1917, asking for the "formation of a flying corps of 4,500 airplanes, personnel and materiel included . . . to be sent to the French front during the campaign of 1918 . . . 2,000 airplanes should be constructed each month, as well as 4,000 engines. . . ."

Ribot concluded his cable with, "The French Government is anxious to know if the American Government accepts this proposition, which would allow the Allies to win supremacy of the air."

In a country absolutely straining to help, the cable could not have been more effective if it had been engraved on tablets of stone. That it was imprecise as to the types or even proportion of types was not important. The Allies wanted aircraft and the U.S. would build them. The cable was referred to the Joint Army-Navy Technical Aircraft Board, which responded on May 29, 1917, with a sober analysis. The Board indicated that meeting the French request, in combination with the known need for training planes and the large requirement for spares, would call for a building program of 22,000 airplanes and 43,800 engines; a staggering total, particularly when contrasted to the pitifully few aircraft the U.S. had built in the past.

As the various boards began to lumber into action, it became imperative to choose which aircraft to manufacture. A decision had been made on May 15, 1917, to send a technical mission to Europe. Headed by Colonel Raynal Cawthorne Bolling, the Commission included some of the brightest young men in military service and industry, as well as 93 competent technicians who were to investigate the details of producing a foreign aircraft.

The Bolling Commission's whirlwind tour of Europe reflected both the enthusiasm of the Americans and the national characteristics of the countries visited. In England the Americans were warmly received, given access to production facilities, and offered full rights to production of aircraft and engines without any more than ordinary commercial considerations The French, in contrast, seemed extraordinarily anxious to drive rapacious bargains and managed in short order to alienate many of the Americans, who, admittedly, brought with them an understandably annoying "we shall win the war for you" attitude. The Italians were initially open and generous but, as time passed, they assumed a fiercely proprietary attitude about their products and were unwilling to relinquish any degree of control over their designs for manufacture in the United States.

There was some inevitable confusion. Initially, orders were placed for Martinside scouts, DH-4s, Spads[5], Capronis, Bristol Fighters, and Handley Page bombers. These orders were shifted about, increased, cancelled, and modified; and all the while, orders for additional indigenous designs—the Standard trainers, Thomas-Morse Scouts, Jennies, and others— were wafted back and forth between the Standard Airplane Company, Fisher Body Company, the Dayton-Wright Airplane Company, Curtiss, and a host of minor organizations.

The desire to place the Liberty engine, in one of its six-, eight- or twelve-cylinder versions, in all of the aircraft added to the complications and resulted in at least one project, the Bristol Fighter, becoming completely useless.

In the end, reason began to prevail, and in a few months a certain pragmatic sense came about. The request for Spad and S.E. 5 fighters was dropped because "monoplace" pursuits could be procured readily in France. The Caproni program crawled on at a snail's pace with the Italians unwilling or unable to come to grips with American production of the aircraft; the

Another posed photo—the young lady second from the right apparently fidgeted a bit. Later shots of the aircraft being restored are not too different.

Propellers were made from carefully selected wood, laminated into blocks, and then profiled to shape, three at a time.

Handley Page program really went rather well, given the difficult task of getting the huge number of drawings converted from English to U.S. practice and then setting up the actual manufacture of the aircraft.

The production problems of the various U.S.-designated aircraft were sorted out, and the DH-4 remained as the sole foreign type to be mass produced. More than 5,000 were ordered from Dayton-Wright, a company just formed in April 1917; another 4,000 were ordered from Fisher; and more than 1,000 from Standard. Many of these would be cancelled, not from any faults of the aircraft but from the happy termination of the war.

de Havilland – The English Origins

The tiny, cultured, accomplished English aviation aristocracy was a remarkable phenomenon; a relatively small number of young men, fascinated by aviation, desiring to make a fortune if possible, but anxious to participate in flight in any event. They proved to be a distinguished, even, to stretch a point, a war-winning combination. Their names, Handley Page, T.O.M. Sopwith, A.V. Roe, and others, became household words, and their products were known and flown worldwide.

None was more distinguished than Geoffrey de Havilland, who, first with the Royal Aircraft Factory and then with The Aircraft Manufacturing Company (Airco), produced many first-rate designs. Slender, wiry, with an intense look, de Havilland had a life highlighted by personal triumphs and saddened by numbing personal tragedies. Two of his sons were killed testing de Havilland aircraft; de Havilland later had to endure the bitter pain associated with the Comet jet airliner disasters in the 1950s.

Yet in those early days, life could not have gone better for young Captain (later Sir) Geoffrey de Havilland. A "motor engineer" at the time of the expansion of the automobile industry in England, de Havilland became absolutely obsessed with aviation. He crashed in his first flight of his own aircraft in December 1909, but pressed on to teach himself to fly in his second airplane in 1910. He soon joined the Army Balloon Factory at Farnborough as a designer and pilot, and there developed the F.E. 1, F.E. 2, B.E. 1, and B.E. 2 aircraft.

He joined the Airco in 1914, and designed a stunning series of airplanes that ultimately constituted one-third of England's entire wartime production of aircraft. (In America, DH's would amount to an even greater percentage of all combat aircraft production.) So pleased with his work was Airco that they did a most un-British thing and designated the company aircraft as de Havillands, much as Focke-Wulf did with Kurt Tank's later designs in World War II.

After World War I, the Stag Lane factory would be the site of numerous civil and military designs, the most famous of which was the de Havilland Mosquito, the almost perfect bomber/fighter/reconnaissance aircraft of World War II of typical de Havilland boldness. More than 23,000 aircraft were manufactured under the de Havilland name plate in World War II.

In World War I, however, the most famous de Havilland design was the D.H.4, his fourth design for Airco, and a complete departure from his previous practice. The D.H.1 had been a two-place pusher that appeared in January 1915. Powered by a 70-horsepower Renault engine, which gave it a very mediocre performance, the D.H.1 never achieved much prominence, but did foster the famous D.H.2, the answer to the "Fokker Scourge." Basically a scaled-down single place D.H.1, the D.H.2 was powered by either a Gnome or Le Rhone rotary engine of 100 to 110 horsepower, and was built in quantity for the time, more than 400 being produced. With its single Lewis gun, the D.H.2 was unquestionably superior to the Fokker Eindecker, and started the see-saw competition of fighter planes that has not ended to this day.

The D.H.3 was a twin-engined biplane carrying gunners both fore and aft of the wings, a formidable defensive arrmament for early 1916. Although only two were built, much of the D.H.3's configuration appeared in the D.H.10 twin-engined bomber of 1918.

To airmen accustomed to flinging themselves against the enemy in BE2s, F.E.8s and other similar crocks, the minor discrepancies of the D.H.4 were as nought. Committed to battle for the first time on April 6, 1917, the day the U.S. entered the war, the D.H.4 fought in France, Italy, Russia, Turkey, Mesopotamia, and over England, the North Sea, and the Aegean Sea. It carried bombs, took photographs and engaged in low-level strafing attacks. Highly successful in reconnaissance, it harassed submarines and even shot down a Zeppelin. When replaced on the production line by the "improved" D.H.9, it went on to rugged service with one squadron of the Independent Force in which it bombed the German heartland (well, as far as Cologne, anyway).

The key to the D.H.4's versatility was its combination of clean lines, generous wing area distributed over rather high aspect ratio surfaces for the day, and the excellent Rolls Royce engine. So valuable that at first the aircraft was not permitted to operate at altitudes under 15,000 feet, the D.H.4 eventually equipped more than 25 squadrons and was recklessly exploited in true Trenchard[6] fashion.

When Rolls Royce ran into production problems, other engines were tried, ranging from the rather anemic 230-horsepower Siddeley Puma through Fiats and Renaults. As they became available, a whole range of Rolls engines were installed. Performance naturally varied; the 230-horsepower Puma engines pushed it to a mere 103 mph at 9,000 feet, while the husky 375-horsepower Rolls-Royce Eagle Mark VIII carried it to 133 mph at the same altitude. Heavily loaded, i.e., with four 112-pound bombs on board, the Puma engine could not crack the 100 mph mark at 13,000 feet.

The total British production of aircraft naturally exceeded that of the United States during the war, the British producing 55,000 and the Americans 14,000. The British rate of production was better than 40,000 aircraft per year in mid-1918, compared to the U.S. rate of 18,700 by November of that year. Thus it is somewhat surprising that there were only 1,449 D.H.4s built by the British, compared to a total of more than 4,000 delivered by U.S. factories by November 30, 1918, and 4,846 by the end of production. The reason was timing; the British had abandoned the D.H.4 in favor of the D.H.9 in late July 1917 in the expectation of better performance. However, the aircraft drawings that were available in the U.S. for the decision in the crucial July/August time period were of the D.H.4. In Britain's case, it was a dreadful mistake: the D.H.9s were being turned out like hot cakes but equipped with the unreliable 230-horsepower B.H.P. engine, and while changing the pilot and fuel tank locations was a great improvement, the plane's performance was inferior to the D.H.4s.

The Liberty Engine

It's really difficult to imagine that the Liberty engine would be shrouded so long in myth. It was produced in great quantity by the United States during World War I and had a distinguished career in half a hundred aircraft types. After the War the engine was used in other capacities (e.g., in military tanks by Great Britain). Yet this is the case with the Liberty engine, about which so much has been written, which has been used by so many famous flyers on so many famous flights, and which nonetheless still wears the uncomfortable mantle of wild, inaccurate press publicity.

The reason for all this, of course, is that while there have been perhaps half a dozen worthwhile articles and books written on the Liberty engine over the years, the number of people who read them was small. On the other hand, the yellow journals that ran the pejorative material on the engine reached millions, and it was in the minds of the general public that the myths were created.

The myths were varied; one, of course, was that the Liberty engine was

Liberty engines were received, inspected, and built up for installations.

Initial engine runup for the engine/ plane combination was in the fuselage; here a Liberty manufactured by the Ford Motor Company is being readied for test.

designed, *ab initio*, in a few days in a hotel room; others were that it was much too heavy; that it was extremely unreliable; that it consumed oil at a prodigious rate; and that it was terribly expensive to operate. There was also a great deal of confusion about the scandals that attended the Liberty plane and the Liberty engine.

The reality is naturally much more prosaic. The Liberty engine was designed in the Willard Hotel in Washington, D.C. in a relatively short period of time, but the whole process was based on a vast amount of experience. It was not too heavy, comparing favorably with the Rolls Royce and Mercedes engines used on the Western Front. It was not too unreliable, even from the beginning, and when given a reasonable development period, became quite reliable, especially at the horsepower ratings that were originally specified. It initially used a great deal of oil, but when an oil was developed for its special use, consumption went down to normal levels for the time. It was not terribly expensive to operate; even ten years after it was produced it compared favorably with the much more modern Curtiss D-12 engines in terms of hourly operating expense, and its initial production costs were less than that of a comparable Rolls Royce engine. As for the scandals, its entire production process was separate from that of the Liberty plane in terms of the manufacturers involved. (There was, of course, an intimate relationship in terms of delivery schedules.)

The reality is actually far more intriguing than the myths; the latter derived from the writing of uninformed reporters, while the former was a triumph of a magnitude that would not be seen again until the second World War.

The wonderful American combination of greed and patriotism came together to make the Liberty engine. Greed is perhaps harsh, for the two men who brought the conceptual essentials of the Liberty engine together, Elbert J. Hall and Jesse G. Vincent, were simply successful engineers in the growing U.S. heavy industry, and they naturally wished to sell their products. It was an unusual situation in which each man brought to the conference table, chaired by Colonel Edwin Deeds, a relatively modern aero engine developed by private industry. Each man provided about half of the ideas that went into the Liberty and each man provided half of the necessary impetus to get the program rolling. Later, Hall would be assigned to other projects and Vincent would become the man associated most closely with the Liberty.

Deeds and S.D. Waldon, both members of the Aircraft Production Board, had decided that the U.S. would not follow the example of France and England and encourage the establishment of a cottage industry of engines, with all of the attendant problems of mass production, spares and so on. (England was producing or experimenting with 37 engines; France was doing the same with 46.) Instead, they determined that a series of engines of substantially the same components, but with more cylinders for added power, would be the best way for the United States to bring its industrial know-how to bear.

These four men, Waldon, Deeds, Vincent, and Hall, would orchestrate an industrial miracle, one which has been largely unappreciated. If they had produced a successful engine over a longer period of time, or if they had produced a less-than-successful engine in the same period of time, it would have been remarkable enough. As it was, they introduced a new and powerful aircraft engine of very modern design into production and into combat in less than fifteen months.

Surfaces were stacked after receiving final doping and insignia. Note wing at center has not had insignia completed.

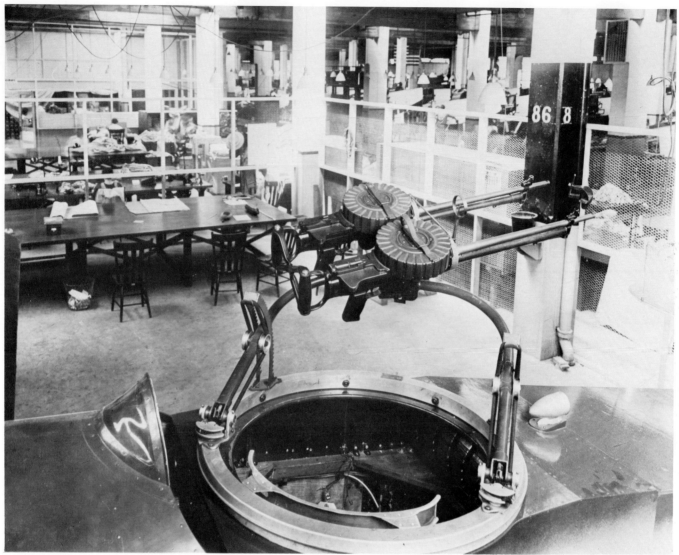

Twin Lewis guns installed on a Scarff ring; this is probably a test installation, as guns were controlled too tightly for casual installation at the plant.

Both Vincent and Hall were in Washington, D.C., to sell their own engines. Vincent had superintended the investment by the Packard Motor Car Company of over $400,000 in a twelve cylinder aircraft engine of about 240 horsepower. Hall had developed an even bigger engine of 450 horsepower that was in the final testing process for his Hall-Scott firm. Both men generously contributed the ideas and experience that had gone into these twin programs when called upon to do so by Deeds.

It had been decided that the U.S.A. Standardized Aircraft Engine, as it was prosaically called, would in fact be a line of 4-, 6-, 8- and 12-cylinder engines developing, respectively, about 100, 215, 270 and 400 horsepower. As things developed, only the 12-cylinder engine was mass produced, because there were adequate substitutes for the 4- and 6-cylinder versions and the 8-cylinder type had an unsolvable vibration problem. To arrive at this stable of engines, Vincent and Hall had been closeted on May 29, 1917, in Deed's hotel suite at the Willard Hotel.

The two men exchanged ideas and systematically called upon available resources in Washington for input. The French Mission gave ideas on the current and future situation at the front, the Society of Automotive Engineers furnished drafting material, the Bureau of Standards provided en-

Fuselages in assembly; note general cleanliness of shop, good lighting, tidy tool benches, etc. This was a first-rate manufacturing organization.

gineering data and Vincent and Hall were the integrating brainpower to distill their experience and their new knowledge of requirements to lay out a proposed design.

Approval for their concepts came on May 31; by June 4, complete layouts had been made; on June 5, the Packard Company agreed to finance the project until the appropriate reimbursement was possible; on June 7, Vincent and Hall departed for Detroit to supervise the actual construction of the engines.

The first 8-cylinder engine was delivered for tests to the Bureau of Standards on July 3, 1917; on August 25, a 12-cylinder Liberty passed a 50-hour test (the British would simply not have believed this to be possible, given their own engine developmental problems) and on August 29, 1917, the number 4 production Liberty engine was flown in the first U.S.-built DH-4. By October 1918, Liberty engines were being built at the rate of 46,000 per year and foreign countries were eagerly competing for delivery schedules. When production ended, 20,478 Liberty engines had been built and they would dominate the field for the next ten years. The automobile industry had responded magnificently to the challenge. Production was as follows: Packard, 6,500; Lincoln, 6,500; Ford, 3,950; General Motors, 2,328, and Nordyke and Marmon, 1,000. The general opinion of the troops in the field was that the Ford-built engines were the best, but this would be very hard to establish as a matter of fact.

The 12-cylinder Liberty engine, despite its firm roots in Vincent and Hall's experience, incorporated a host of modern features, some of which gave rise to later criticism. The crankcase was split along the horizontal center line and the two pieces were fastened together with bolts running from top to bottom. The cylinders were set at an angle of 45 degrees rather than the customary 60 degrees and were similar to those used by the Mercedes. A most unusual departure was the use of Delco battery ignition instead of the conventional magneto type; no adequate magnetos were available at the time and the Delco system made the big Liberty relatively easy to start. Alumi-

Equipment installation in the unfinished fuselage; this looks like a dummy installation for the radio.

31

num pistons were a relative novelty, as was the extent to which the cylinders were encased by a water jacket for cooling. One obsolete feature, later changed, was the scupper system of lubrication; it was adequate for power output of up to about 350 horsepower, but beyond that point there was a need for pressurized lubrication.

Like most of the engines of the day, the Liberty combined large cubic displacement with a relatively low compression ratio and low RPM to achieve its design horsepower. The basic engine weighed 786 pounds, but the normal powerplant installation, including radiator, and fluids, weighed over 900 pounds.

Liberty was developed continuously during its limited production life, as information flowed back from its service use. As a practical matter, however, production was discontinued in March 1919 before a great deal of service experience was gained. In the next five years new concepts of ignition, lubrication, and vibration dampening were incorporated in the almost 12,000 engines that were in stock. In addition, there was an unending series of experiments with turbosuperchargers, controllable pitch propellers, and other devices. Even the basic design of the engine would be changed so that it could be operated inverted or even aircooled. The Allison engines, which were the United States' most modern liquid-cooled engine in World War II, derived from such experimentation with the Liberty.

After the war the engine was used in everything from modified DH-4s, to rum-running boats, to wind machines on Hollywood sets. It was used as a tank engine in Russia and was adopted for manufacture by Great Britain for use in their Cruiser and Crusader tanks.

The Air Service, and later the Air Corps, relied upon the stocks of Liberties to power observation and bomber planes until July 1, 1929, when the Chief of the Air Corps finally forbade its use in any further new aircraft. It had become, not unnaturally, an inhibiting design factor, for just as the price of new bombers has kept the B-52 in service, so did the price of new engines keep the "free" Liberty engines attractive. In its ten-year period of

All major events wre well publicized at Dayton-Wright; here the fuselage of "Ship No. 1,000" is in the process of assembly, on July 24, at 2:00 PM.

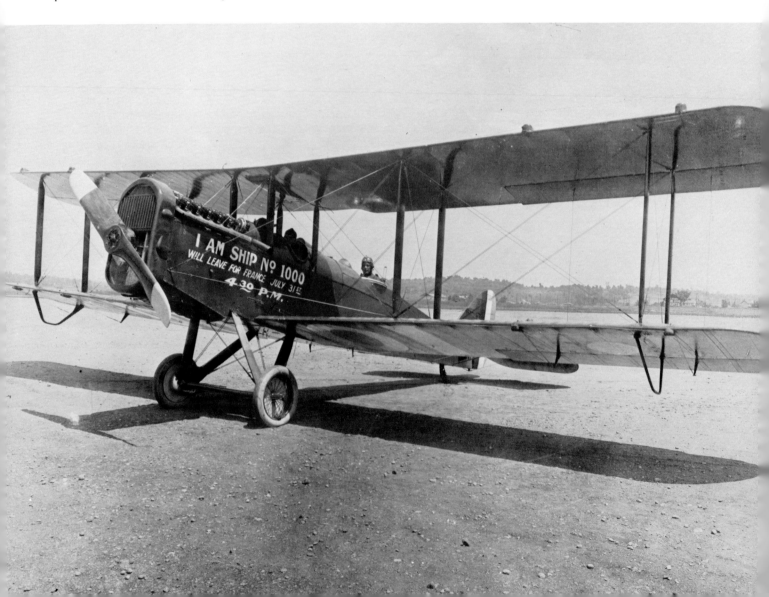

Later that day assembly of the plane was further along, awaiting engine installation.

On July 31, the aircraft was fully assembled for its final test. Note quality of workmanship, the "1,000" painted in reverse on lower wing.

ascendancy, however, it powered such important aircraft as the Douglas World Cruisers, the Curtiss NC-4, the Fokker T-2, the Martin and Huff-Daland bombers, and a whole host of observation types. It was ubiquitous.

Its ubiquity served the National Air and Space Museum as late as 1978. Western Air Lines had restored a Douglas M-2 mail plane and decided to fly it across country for its formal donation to the Museum. Over Amarillo Airport, pilot Don Lykins heard an explosion as the pistons and cylinders of his aged Liberty engine went through the cowling. He made an emergency landing at the airport, and it seemed like the last part of the journey to the Smithsonian would be made by truck. Almost unbelievably, however, Lykins knew that only about a hundred miles away was a brand new, zero-time Liberty engine, still in its crate. The owners generously offered to trade the engine. Within 48 hours an engine change had been made and the lovely old biplane continued its cross-country journey to its destination in the Hall of Air Transportation. Once again the Liberty engine had been ready.

The Liberty Plane

The production of the American version of the D.H.4 got under way under the most adverse possible conditions and was brought to fruition only by a combination of unusual circumstances, hard-working people, and the general fervid patriotism of the time. There were a hundred factors that could have totally subverted the program, from inept management to faulty design of airplane or engine. (Other engine programs—the Wright-Martin version of the Hispano, the Bugatti, the Gnome Rhones—ran the gamut from moderate success to abysmal catastrophe.)

These were all to be produced by American firms with a competence equivalent to those that produced the Liberty. A major difference, of course, was the fact that the Liberty was American-designed, while all of the others had to be adapted from foreign sources.

The entire American warplane production program was very brief, only 19 months from conception to cancellation, and the circumstances prevailing were totally unfavorable for its success. Yet it happened that at Dayton-Wright, where the largest production contract was placed, the situation was right.

The history of this company had begun earlier in 1916, when Charles F. "Boss" Kettering, a man who measured his patents not by numbers but by how many inches high they stacked each year, met with Orville Wright. Wright had recently sold his interests in the original Wright Airplane Company to a group that ultimately became Wright-Martin and retained his name and the services of Glenn L. Martin. Kettering persuaded the "father of aviation" to join with him and the Harold Talbotts, father and son, who were powers in the local banking industry, in establishing a private aeronautical laboratory to be called the Wright Field Company.

The first challenge of the new firm was the design of a safe aircraft for training pilots, and this was called, somewhat engagingly, the FS, for "first shot." Designed by Orville Wright and Louis C. Lueneke, this little-known airplane was flown only eight weeks after construction started and, unlike almost all of its contemporaries, could not be spun. Powered by a Hall-Scott engine of 110 horsepower, its speed range was a creditable 35 to 68 mph. Later re-engined with a 150-horsepower Hisso, its rate of climb went up remarkably, but the speed increased only to about 85 mph. The airplane was test flown at the old Wright field, which subsequently became known as McCook Field. Two airplanes were made, the second somewhat unimaginatively being called FS-2, or "first shot, no.2."

The design was immediately tendered to the Army in the hopes of a production contract, but it was not accepted on the basis that there were not adequate drawings. Drawings, or the lack of them, would plague the company again and again.

On April 9, 1917, three days after the declaration of war, the group met again in Talbott's bank office and raised their sights. They dissolved the Wright Field Company and in its place formed the Dayton-Wright Airplane Company. "Boss" Kettering and Orville were consulting engineers and both

The DH-4s were boxed for overseas shipment with great efficiency. Here fuselage and coaming sections are formed into a unit.

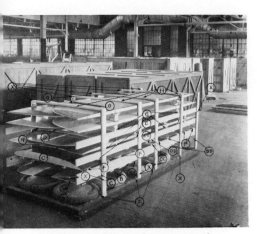

A very complete packing manual, still extant, showed just how to join part D with part N, and remove brace X from Stud Z, etc. Several aircrat components were combined to use all the available space; note there are eight wheels in this pallet.

Right: Aileron shipping rig.

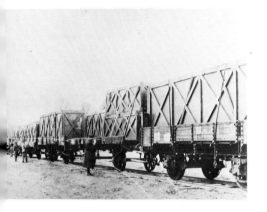

Above: Off-loading in France.

Right: Fuselage box; note stub "propeller" used as brace.

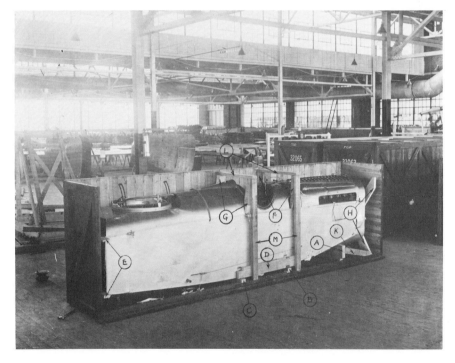

maintained this role throughout the controversial history of Dayton-Wright. The Talbotts were the active managers, as well as providers of extensive financial services.

In 1917, Dayton was to aircraft production what a petri dish culture is to bacteria. An almost laboratory condition prevailed in terms of managerial talent, finance, production space, available skilled labor, and numerous specialty manufacturers. All were ready when the time for production arrived.

One of the group's major interests, the Domestic Engineering Company, which made Delco lighting equipment for farmers, had just completed a mammoth 270-foot-by-1000-foot factory building. It was immediately designated to be the main airplane factory building; its long bays were ideally suited for the mass production of the aircraft of the time. Later, as production demands mounted, it was expanded to more than twice this size.

Even while such large-scale preparations were under way, a curious sense of paternalism managed to survive and prosper. Modern houses were constructed near the plant for sale or rent at subsidized prices; the workrooms, restrooms and other facilities were established in numbers not customarily encountered in American industry at the time. There were even provisions made for a home in Dayton where young women could safely find temporary living accommodations until they could make other arrangements. The concern for morale went so far as the establishment of commissaries for low cost meals, provision for lectures and concerts, band music, and even an entire educational system called the "Dayton Industrial Institute." This far-seeing concept provided schools for upgrading the skills of the labor force to meet aircraft production requirements. All in all, it was a phenomenon rarely seen in American industry, and was almost never carried out with the same care and to the same degree of success.

With the "first shot" rejected, Dayton-Wright anxiously wanted to build other aircraft, and the first order from the Signal Corps was for Curtiss JN-4s. A whole series of drawings arrived, all for different models, and after an immense amount of effort to rationalize the confusion, twenty-five sets of wooden parts were released for production, only to have the Army announce that they were done from the incorrect plans. It didn't really matter much, for the JN-4 order was revoked and instead an order was placed for 400 Standard J-1s to be produced in four months.

There were no adequate lumber stocks on hand, so the initial Dayton-Wright efforts were spent in building dry kilns and acquiring trees and a lumber mill. Linen for covering was soon unobtainable and mercerized cotton fabric had to be substituted.

Despite help from Charles Healy Day, the Standard's designer and a man about whom far too little has been written, it took eight months rather than four to deliver the order. By this time, the production process for the Liberty plane was well underway.

The experience with building the J-1s, traumatic and difficult as it proved to be, was invaluable for the later DH-4 programs, in which almost all the difficulties—poor plans, lack of materials, conflicting instructions, etc.— were repeated, but for which solutions were already known.

On August 14, 1917, Dayton-Wright was selected to manufacture the DH-4. Sample drawings were available, and the Army had been foresighted enough to ship a complete, British-built D.H.4, sans engine, as a sample.

The momentum of the Standard program immediately served Dayton-Wright well. Drawings for 35,330 different components, including 2,608 wood parts, 1,665 sheet metal parts, 20 forgings, 366 pieces of fabric, 474 items of equipment, and 343 miscellaneous parts were scrutinized and corrected. Many parts were completely redesigned, and in all cases dimensions had to be converted not only from English to American measurements, but also from English to American manufacturing philosophy. The English, with their tradition of craftsmanship, still worked to a system of "fits," to match parts together. The Americans, in the finest Henry Ford tradition, worked with a system of "tolerances," which was much less demanding of the worker on the floor, but much more demanding of the original drawings, jigs, and tools.

Three talented people accompanied the sample D.H.4 from England. George Hancock was shop superintendent for Airco, while Mr. Chapman was an expert on maintenance; his wife was a W.A.A.C., and an expert in quality control of D.H.4s. All three were significant contributors to the successful adaptation of the D.H.4.

The aircraft from England was torn down, photographed and analyzed, with drawings made every step of the way. The first aircraft, virtually handbuilt, was substantially complete by September 1917 and made its first flight on October 29.

It would be well to put to rest the long suspicion that the National Air and Space Museum's DH-4 airplane was in fact the British sample that had been adapted for the Liberty engine. There is ample documentary and physical evidence that this is not so, the most conclusive of which is the use of clearly American made metal fittings throughout the aircraft. There are numerous equally significant clues, including the stamped part numbers, revised placement of fuel tanks, etc..

The people at Dayton-Wright were sufficiently sophisticated, however, not to standardize production on this number one aircraft; instead, they designated the number thirty airplane as the standard for production, realizing full well that in the initial build-up to production there would be many changes.

Accounts of the first flight of the original prototype are so hair-raising that they seem almost apocryphal. Howard Rinehart, a large, likable man who contributed much to aviation and to Dayton-Wright, reportedly took the plane up on its initial flight and proceeded to wring it out with rolls, loops and other maneuvers. A Dayton-Wright employee, Archie Freeman, rode in the gunner's compartment. During inverted flight, the woodscrews holding his seat stripped and Freeman almost fell out. Even if not 100% accurate, it is an extremely entertaining reminiscence about the first flight of an important aircraft. In any event, the fabrication of a formidable airplane like the DH-4 in a little over 90 days was remarkable, even given the fact that plans and a sample copy were furnished.

The initial burst of speed in production was offset by several months of delays when, in usual bureaucratic fashion, there were a series of changes dictated in features such as armament and instrumentation. The major difficulty was in resolving the armament question.

The U.S. Army specified the use of two Marlin machine guns for the forward armament which, in itself, was not a problem but which caused difficulties with cartridge ejection and the Constantinesco synchronizing gear that took months to overcome. In addition, there were many minor changes, all of which took time to agree upon, create and release drawings, and then manufacture the parts.

The installation of two fixed guns, ammunition boxes and a gun mount rigid enough to withstand recoil forces was a challenge. The shell and the clip chutes for the right gun had to be routed around the rear center section strut and still not jam. A clever tinsmith created a large "Dutchman Breeches" shell chute that worked very well.

Another problem area was cooling. The original British radiator was designed for engines in the 250- to 300-horsepower range and the Liberty was half again as large. Not only was the radiator undersized, but there was a mismatch in the water flow rate set by the engine coolant pump and the radiator's ability to handle it. Improper air recirculation in the region swept by the propeller was also troublesome.

A whole series of cut and try experiments resulted in a radiator four inches longer than before, with a different internal circulation system. The

South field, where the experiemtal work was done for Dayton-Wright.

The museum's DH-4, the first DH-4 built by Dayton-Wright, in company with the Dayton-Wright "Messenger." This aircraft is often referred to as a predecessor of the Sperry "Messenger" concept; it was not, being instead a test bed for the little Lawrance engine used on the Kettering "Bug." The Lawrance led to radials, which in turn led to the Wright Whirlwinds and Pratt & Whitney Wasps of little more than a decade later.

initial solution, installed on the Museum's aircraft, consisted of an overhead surge tank and a pipe connection to the header tank of the radiator. The Army regarded this as too vulnerable to gunfire and too dangerous if holed.

Along with the problems that might be expected, there were others that suddenly surfaced as potential production line catastrophes and which had to be solved on the spot by the line engineers. A typical example involved the use of swaged tie rods and fork ends, a method of assembly not previously used in the United States but favored in England. Dayton Metal Products undertook the challenge and adapted standard machinery to create the fittings. Similar difficulties were encountered with fabricating the wire eye-splices used by the British. A training program of local Dayton women was quickly introduced and resulted in a satisfactory solution until new methods were devised.

While the production process was gaining speed, Dayton-Wright experimented with its pre-production aircraft and made a series of comparisons with a British-built D.H.4. It was found that while American methods had actually reduced the all-up weight of the airframe slightly, additional fuel and armament had raised the gross weight, a practice that was to become common to most combat machines when the military increased its requirements.

The actual variances between American and British version were these:

1. The American structure was 66.7 pounds lighter than the British.
2. The 375-horsepower Eagle VIII Rolls Royce engine was 12 pounds lighter than the 400-horsepower Liberty.

Five production DH-4s; the one in the center, the "Humdinger," has a Rolls Royce Eagle engine installed for comparison purposes.

3. The British fuel and oil group was 127.3 pounds lighter than the American.

4. The British armament group was 84.2 pounds lighter than the American.

So, while American methods managed to save 54.7 pounds net on the engine and airframe in what were to become traditional American patterns, they added 211.5 pounds in increased fuel and armament. Considering the usual upward spiral relationship between extra fuel and structural weight, this is really quite remarkable and a tribute to both the original British design and the American modifications.

Dayton-Wright also conducted tests of a stock production Dayton-Wright-built DH-4 and a stock production Fisher-built DH-4. In a long series of intensive tests comparing speed, climb, fuel consumption, and other performance parameters, over a series of measured courses at altitude intervals of two thousand feet from sea level up to the service ceilings, it was found that the two planes were for all practical purposes identical, with any differences in performance stemming from the different propellers with which they were equipped. The Fisher-built aircraft was faster near the ground; they were nearly equal at 10,000 feet, and the Dayton-Wright DH-4 was faster at 15,000 feet. For each condition the faster aircraft was generating more RPM, and hence more power. The test also pointed out the need for better carburetion control to adjust for changes in altitude.

The prototype DH-4 that started it all first appeared in 1916, an amazing aircraft for its time. British aircraft were very similar in appearance to later American versions, but differed considerably in detail.

A not uncommon situation for the DH-4; spots in the mud indicate where it dug in and flipped over.

Not wishing to miss a bet, one final variation was tested. A standard Dayton-Wright-built DH-4 was fitted with a Rolls-Royce Eagle engine. It was officially called the DH-4RR and unofficially christened the "Humdinger." When the somewhat reluctant English test pilot, Captain William Hannay, asked what "Humdinger" meant, he was told, with rather coarse, broad midwestern humor that "A Humdinger is a guy who can take a deaf and dumb girl out and make her say 'Atta Boy'." Hannay's reported reply, probably accurate and certainly apposite, was "Oh, now, I say." Hannay was apparently not enamored of flying and as soon as the war was over made a grateful transfer back to the cavalry.

The Rolls powered DH-4RR was lighter and climbed better than the standard Liberty-powered version, but the latter was slightly faster.

There were perhaps more variations in performance among the Liberty engines than there were between the airframes supplied by the seven different manufacturers. Of this, more later.

In early 1918, all of the various elements incident to volume aircraft production at Dayton-Wright began to come together. Nine were delivered in February, four in March, 15 in April and, finally in May the first sizable batch, 153. Unfortunately, at this same time the paper-thin temper of the American press and public wore through, partially because an over-enthusiastic publicity campaign by Dayton-Wright and the Air Service had tossed off some pitiful half-truths about aircraft deliveries, but more importantly because of a totally spurious campaign waged by Gutzon Borglum, the famous sculptor who carved the monumental figures at Mount Rushmore.

The first element, the publicity brouhaha, stemmed from the Air Service's and Dayton-Wright's desperate desire to get an aircraft enroute to France prior to January 1, 1918. They did, but, in the manner typical of production companies all over the world, cloaked this near-accomplishment in hyperbole. The aircraft that was supposed to be on its way was not entirely complete, and it was on its way only by virtue of being hustled out of the factory late on the night of December 31, 1917. Subsequently, it was determined that it was held up at the port for several weeks and the whole American DH-4 production program was smeared with a poor image.

The Borglum incident was entirely different. Borglum, a senior official in

A famous photo, showing Howard "Sunshine" Rinehart and his most distinguished passenger, Orville Wright. Airplanes had come a long way in just 15 years.

THE DAYTON WRIGHT AIRPLANE CO., SOUTH FIELD - MAY 14-18.

the Ku Klux Klan, made a series of wild charges of treason and inefficiency and secured from President Wilson an unofficial charter, later rued by the administration, to investigate the "airplane mess."

Borglum's charges were aired by the New York *World*; he charged a complete failure of the entire aircraft production program, and he undertook a specific campaign against Colonel E.A. Deeds, who was depicted as a profiteering pro-German whose real name was Dietz.

A less prejudiced investigation revealed that Borglum had a personal hatred of Deeds and that he himself was trying desperately to set himself up as an aircraft manufacturer on the basis of his own design for a (presumably streamlined) airplane, called variously a "fish" or "tube" type, and which he said could lay waste to Germany. His value to the syndicate being formed to manufacture the aircraft was his claimed close friendship with the President.

The Scarff ring made a dandy camera mount. Rinehart in the front cockpit, cameraman is unidentified.

THE DAYTON WRIGHT AIRPLANE CO, SOUTH FIELD - MAY 14-18.

Borglum's accusations were quickly discounted and he was mildly chastised by President Wilson and asked to turn over any material his "investigation" had uncovered to the official investigation.

Even though Borglum was almost immediately recognized as a fraud with a grievous conflict of interest of his own, he set in train a series of investigations that resulted in the history of the entire aviation program being clouded forever. The reputations of men like Deeds, Vincent, and others were, of course, irreparably harmed.

In retrospect, there is no doubt that all of the principals involved in the Dayton-Wright Company and in the design of the Liberty engine were terribly close, and that most had had some sort of business and friendly relations going back over the years. The distinction between government business and friendship must occasionally have blurred. But there is almost no reason to believe that any of the principals involved benefitted in any illegal way from the great sums of money that were being generated. Most, if not all of them were public-spirited citizens who were doing their patriotic duty. Deeds had made full disclosure of his holdings and in general had done more than most public officials did at the time to avoid the appearance of conflict of interest. Still, it was an extremely close-knit group, and one would be surprised if helpful information had not been dispensed in some private conversation, if only by the lift of an eyebrow or a shrug of shoulders. They were, after all, only human, and they had been brought up in the rather freebooting mold of turn-of-the-century industrialists.

The production impetus at Dayton-Wright was underway, however, and the spate of bad publicity did nothing to stop its really impressive climb. Total deliveries were as follows: June, 336; July, 480; August, 124; September, 518; October, 556 and November 504. The 1,000th aircraft from Dayton-Wright was identified on the line in July and an alert public affairs staff followed it through until its shipment to France in large, well-designed boxes. (Noted aviation historian, writer, builder, designer, collector, Peter M. Bowers says that his father remembered seeing these DH-4 boxes, the airplanes still inside them, being lowered into the mud in France to form a platform over which more boxes of DH-4s could be transported to the assembly depot.)

The whole production process at Dayton-Wright was characterized by an amazing combination of extremely modern techniques coupled to a 19th-century production environment. For example, there was a very sophisticated system for finding problems in the field and reporting them back to the production centers, much in the manner that operational hazard reports were filed in the Air Force during and after World War II, or, as modern information management systems work today. It was simple enough; the system was broken down into major components, such as the fuselage, engine, etc. There was a column that identified the source of the complaint and date, a column for the criticism, and a column detailing the correction, as in the following examples.

The bulletins are worth quoting at some length for they reveal as much about the technical organization of the time as they do about the aircraft. It is interesting to note that there were provisions to incorporate suggestions arising from the British experience and that they could be applied across the board to all American manufacturers of DH-4s. The problem of configuration control by careful drawing control procedures is alluded to. The reports reveal concern for morale of the workers, as well as the need for being more demanding. In other reports there are also references to the establishment of international standards for certain materials and components, as well as for fasteners.

GENERAL

By Whom Date	CRITICISM	CORRECTION
Capt. Frank Burton 7/30/18		General. There has been a certain amount of laxity in inspection on these planes with the result that bolts are sometimes not provided with nuts, the empennage and aileron hinges have excessive play, cable terminals have been wrapped and soldered while so dirty that the solder did not stick, and internal wooden members of the wing construction sometimes do not fit as well as they should. These points can be remedied only by careful inspection and great stress should be laid upon the need of this inspection without however criticizing too severely the work which has already been done.
Memo from Mr. McClelland 7/3/18	Dayton Wright & Standard furnishing 66-gallon tank; Fisher-Body, 88-gallon tanks as soon as they can get them. All will be changed when electric-driven tank comes in production.	O.K. on Standard & Fisher planes. Dayton-Wright production to carry 88-gallon tanks beginning about July 25.
Cable #1361 6/24/18	Water pipe from bottom radiator to pump should be moved to starboard to clear oil strainers.	Col. Hall has been directed to take up this matter personally with Col. Dodd in France (see answer to Cable 1361-Par. Sub-Paragraph 6).
Cable #1361 6/24/18	Vent for radiators must have a tube leading water where it can not blow on spark plug or pilot & vent should not be in radiator caps.	This fault has been corrected at all Plants.
Cable #1361 6/24/18	Wrapping of wire terminals in some cases bad.	Every effort being made to improve this. One man being delegated to follow this exclusively. Trouble will be stopped by rigid enforcement of a definite specification covering materials and processing of soldering.
Cable #1361 6/24/18	Liberty Motor is defective, indicating shop inspection not satisfactory. Lincoln apparently better than Packard.	
Memo from Mr. McClelland. 7/3/18	Eleven different makes of radiators now being tested. All have different types of cores, with same outside dimensions. Attempt being made to obtain radiator which is more satisfactory without changing design and construction of front end fuselage, which would interfere seriously with production.	Designs not completed Promised July 22.
Capt. Frank Burton 7/30/18		Recently the British DH-4 squadrons have been experiencing considerable trouble due to the bracing wire which terminates in the top longerons of the engine section pulling these longerons up and doing extensive damage to the entire fuselage at this point. They have remedied the matter by continuing these wires to the lower longeron just back of the radiator and fastening them to the fixture now holding the forward landing wires. At the point where the wires pass the top longeron there should be a bracket to hold the wire away from the exhaust pipes. While we have not experienced any difficulty from this source up to the present, we may encounter it later when we have made a large number of landings with our planes. The change is very easily made and cannot help but be advantageous.

ARMAMENT
Guns

By Whom Date	CRITICISM	CORRECTION
Lt. Walter J. Seahorn 8/3/18		An expert on Marlin Guns should be sent to Ourches, and kept there until this question is settled. Much depends upon the success of the first squadron and too much trouble cannot be taken to give them assistance.

MOTOR - Accessories, etc.

By Whom Date	CRITICISM	CORRECTION
Lt. Col. H. Dunwoody 7/31/18		The chief faults of the engine itself are noted as follows: Material not up to specifications, bad workmanship, negligent inspection and careless assembly have been noted in say 15% of the engines. This figure is a fairly close estimate, and should be taken to show that a considerable percentage of the engines will very quickly be damaged, if not wrecked, due to initial defects which might have been prevented by using more care in manufacture in the United States. Such preliminary overhaul and inspection has actually been made on many of the engines received here, and it proves to be almost as necessary for engines recently received as for those which arrived in the first shipments. But with the limited number of mechanics available here, we must take chances and put many of the engines into flying service without inspection. MORE RIGID INSPECTION IN THE U.S. IS REQUIRED.
Lt. Col. H. Dunwoody 7/31/18		Certain faults in design of the engine accessories must positively be remedied as quickly as possible. Note the following: The oil tank is too small. At the end of the longest flight it is not safe to have less than say three gallons remaining in the tank (because of contamination and heating). Because the tank is so small, the mechanics are of course likely to fill it full, yet if filled full or nearly full, it is almost certain to be burst when the engine starts. The filler for the oil tank should be two inches in diameter. The drain should be a ¾ inch plug cock, *not* a ¼ inch pipe plug. The inlet and outlet pipes between the oil tank and oil pump, including entrances to the pump, should be not less than 1 inch in diameter. (This is important.) The new U.S. D-9-A, with 140 gallon gas tank should have a 12 gallon oil tank. The water hose connections at the pump outlets are not safe. On engines now complete a different form of hose band should be supplied, and on future engines the hose should have a longer bearing on the metal tubes over which it slips.

In traditional military style, there were various boards of officers delegated to approve, reject, or modify suggested changes, much in the manner of modern configuration control boards. At Romaratin, France, a typical meeting from August 22 to 24 furnished an eight-page report covering everything from propeller hub shims to packing the ailerons more securely in the shipping boxes.

The existence of such procedures and boards is commonplace today, but they were radical innovations at a time when the Air Service had expanded from 260 officers to almost nine times that number in a little over 18 months. The logistic difficulties—recruiting, training, and assignment of tasks—were overwhelming and were solved only by the same thing that drove DH-4 production to such heights at home: patriotism, commitment, youthful enthusiasm and the lack of red tape to inhibit the process. The latter was probably the most significant, for the services grew, like production, faster than the bureaucracy that would have inevitably hampered them.

Development went on at home, too. The need for self-sealing tanks was terribly evident and Dayton-Wright pursued two separate methods. One involved wrapping a thick, soft rubber jacket over the regular fuel tank, with an inner wall of insulation of about two inches of sawdust. The object was to not seal the tank so much as to prevent air mixing with escaping gasoline to form an explosive vapor. The other method, which subsequently was adopted for use by the RAF as the Imber tank, and which was similar to other tanks developed for use in World War II, consisted of vulcanizing to the outside of the fuel tank a half-cooked shell of uncured rubber. A bullet passing through this mixture would cause fuel to leak onto the rubber, which would react and seal up the hole.

The Dayton-Wright complex soon settled into an almost routine process of building, testing and shipping DH-4s to the front. The first aircraft that arrived were not nearly so well put together as the later ones, for there was a tremendous amount of learning to be done. However, as time passed, skills and quality improved. The testing was done routinely but not without hazard, for many of the test pilots were newly trained themselves and totally unaware of the hazards inherent in flying a brand new combat aircraft.

As DH-4 production reached record levels, the Army Air Service presented Dayton-Wright with a wonderful solution to the DH-4/D.H.9 controversy. At McCook Field, a series of original aircraft had been built, including the rather elegant U.S.A.C.-1, but the successor to the DH-4 was to be the USD-9, a modified version of the de Havilland D.H.9 to be powered by the Liberty, of course.

Dayton-Wright was disconcerted by a proposal for 1,000 USD-9As to be delivered during the first six weeks of 1919, at a time when the firm still had thousands of DH-4s to complete. Dayton-Wright and Curtiss were both to manufacture the aircraft, and they examined the drawings from McCook Field with great interest. The first thing they noticed was that despite the apparent similarity to the American DH-4 in general appearance, there was almost no commonality of jigs, parts, tools, drawings, or metal fittings. In their desire to produce a new airplane, no one had taken into consideration the enormous foundation already laid with the DH-4 production.

Dayton-Wright management steamed and schemed; there was no way they could comply with the new production schedule. Instead, they devised a counter offer: they would meet the intended design requirements of the D.H.9/USD-9A by incorporating the necessary features into a new airplane, the DH-4B. They began making layouts, including a one-quarter scale drawing of the new aircraft, with all parts common to the previous DH-4 in black, and the parts of the DH-4B in red—and there was suprisingly little red.

*A DH-4 built by the Standard
Aeroplane Corporation. Note the
difference in the shop equipment
compared to the Dayton-Wright plant.*

Kettering briefed the representatives of the Aircraft Production Board, from McCook Field and elsewhere, and with little opposition got a complete approval. The USD-9 disappeared into oblivion. Ultimately, after much negotiation, the firm delivered 200 DH-4Bs.

The armistice brought with it the natural mixed feelings about shutting down a vibrant new industry. Still, Daytonians were nothing if not optimistic, and it wouldn't be long before Dayton-Wright would blossom forth with a whole new series of new designs, many based on the DH-4, of course. The determination of their success or failure would lie in the market place, a familiar arena where the men who had created Dayton-Wright had almost never failed.

The Liberty Plane at War

On February 20, 1918, the internationally famous Lafayette Escadrille (Spa. 124 of the French Air Force) formally became the 103rd Aero Squadron of the United States Army Air Service, and was the only American air unit actively engaged in combat. On March 15, unarmed Nieuport 28s of the 95th Aero Squadron made their first tentative patrols over the front, in company with French Spads from Villeneuve-les-Vertus. From this point on, there began a tremendous build up in the U.S. fighting strength: There were five squadrons by June 1, 13 by July, 16 in August, 24 in September, 30 in October and 36 by November first. On November 11, 1918, there were 740 aircraft at the front. Of these, 328 were Spad fighters, 157 Salmsons, 196 DH-4s, 43 Breguets, 12 Sopwith Camels, and 4 S.E.5s.

Of the DH-4s, 80 were day bombers attached to the First Army, while 116 were observation planes attached to the Second Army. When the war ended, the U.S. DH-4 had been engaged in combat for only 70 days, but had established itself as an excellent fighting plane, far more useful as an observation type than as a bomber.

The first group of four U.S. DH-4s arrived in France on May 6, 1918, and was sent to the Air Service Production Center No. 2 at Romorantin. The first was assembled and test flown on May 17 by Captain B.R. Osborne, Commanding Officer of the Villacoublay detachment, amid suitable publicity. As indicated earlier, however, the aircraft arriving from the United States were still suffering from their manufacturer's lack of experience and with many problems still to be corrected.

An experienced RAF pilot, Captain Hucks, test flew the aircraft on May 30th and wrote up a number of alarming deficiencies. He noted that the tail was badly fitted and showed considerable looseness when shaken, due to the fact that wood screws had been used in many places instead of nuts and bolts. The airspeed indicator seemed to read about 50% low, as the maximum speed indication he could obtain was 60 mph. Captain Hucks was bothered by the fact that the radiator threw out water during his entire flight, even though the temperature had not reached the boiling point, and by the fact that the gasoline line ("petrol pipe") to the carburetor was routed beneath the exhaust manifold, hardly a good practice.

There were numerous problems with this and succeeding aircraft and the American air depot grew from a pine forest in January to a massive industrial establishment with more than 2,800,000 square feet of building area, seven miles of roads, 10 miles of railroads and 425 acres of flying fields. Over 12,000 officers and soldiers were employed and 1,101 were doing DH-4 assembly when the war ended. So rapid had been the growth in size that even the boxes that the DH-4s arrived in were converted to temporary barracks to help ease the housing shortage.

The 135th Aero Squadron at Ourches was among the first to receive the new Liberty planes, and early in August the first mission was flown "by American pilots, in American planes, powered by American engines." The exact date is variously given as August 2, 7, 8, or 9 (the last date is probably

When the DH-4s arrived in France,
they were received with appropriate
christening ceremonies. This photo is
captioned as "First Flight of the
Liberty Plane." Representatives of the
allied countries and welfare workers
at the christening before the flight.

Lined up for the first combat sortie,
August 9, 1918. Not a bad way to
take off if you have sufficient field
ahead for the first plane.

This is a rather bizarrely painted DH-4 with a 345 horsepower Rolls Royce Eagle engine.

A DH-4 of the U.S. Marine Corps, 1918. The crew is unfortunately not identified.

correct). It really doesn't matter much from a military point of view, but as propaganda, it was a smashing success.

Eighteen (some accounts say 16 and a photo shows 16) Liberty planes were lined up, nose to tail, with Brigadier General Benjamin D. Foulois, Chief of Air Service, in the lead plane, piloted by 1st Lt. A. Blair Thaw. With cameras rolling, the formation trundled off single-file from the field into murky weather that caused the unit soon to break up, with no airplane penetrating further than Nancy, a considerable distance behind the front lines. The lack of concrete results did not matter, for the morale effect was tremendous.

After so many recent years of American predominance in the air, it is a

51

DH-4s of the 168th Aero Squadron.

Aircraft of the 1105th School Squadron.

little difficult to recall that there was only one uniform characteristic that permeated the U.S. Army Air Service from its commander to the lowliest private, and that was inexperience. While the U.S. had had observers at the front, and while there had been Americans serving in Allied units, there was no solid core of experience. Figuratively as well as literally, the Air Service was winging it.

The first weeks at the front were a crash course in combat, where mistakes were often made and quickly learned from. For example, the DH-4s were at first assigned as "fighters" to act as top cover for Spads doing ground attack work. The problems in assembly and the unsuitability of the DH-4 for the task was evident on the first attempt, and the tactic was abandoned. And, although the Yanks had gone through the same schools as their British and French allies, it took practical experience to make things work. During the first observation sorties, inexperienced pilots and observers would sometimes fail to report targets of opportunity directly to the artillery posts so that immediate fire could be directed. Instead, they followed the school solution for work, noting and recording the information, then transmitting it to corps headquarters for retransmission down the chain of command, while the artillery commanders waxed furious. The new bomber squadrons had more to learn, and more to suffer. The fully loaded DH-4 was far more vulnerable to attack, particularly to the new Fokker D VII fighters that were beginning to replace Albatros and Pfalz types. In training, the aircraft the U.S. pilots had flown were lightly loaded and had a reserve of power that enabled the inexperienced pilots to maintain formation readily. In combat the overladen DH-4 was at full throttle almost all of the time, and station keeping was difficult. Similarly, observers had trained on aircraft equipped with only one Lewis gun; the twin-gun installation used in combat was unfamiliar, and resulted in some self-inflicted damage to the tail as wires were shot away.

But war is a swift educator, and in a matter of weeks the DH-4 units had settled into a routine that belied the fact that six months earlier the equipment had not existed, nor had the men been trained.

The lessons learned paid off quickly. During the Meuse-Argonne offensive

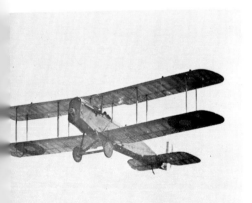

In flight, the DH-4 had a fragile, airy appearance due to the translucence of the fabric and the delicate tracery of construction. Note the position of the insignia, outboard on the wings. (Peter M. Bowers Collection)

that began on September 26, squadrons combined to mount formations of 16 to 18 aircraft, and these proved far less vulnerable to attack. Piloting, bombing, and observation skills had gone up sharply as well, and the units gave an excellent accounting of themselves. The period was also marked by a decline in German aggressiveness, as the war now appeared to be headed for its conclusion.

During 1918, there were many individual instances of heroism, some well-known and documented, others simply the anonymous fare of the soldier.

The single most famous incident was, of course, the brave efforts to resupply the immortal "LOST BATTALION" by 1/Lt. Harold E. Goettler and 2nd Lt. Erwin R. Bleckley of the 50th Aero Squadron. A battalion of the 77th Division had been cut off in the Argonne Forest. The two young men had already made one resupply trip earlier that afternoon through intense German rifle and machine gun fire.

Goettler brought the DH-4 in low and fast in the hopes that Bleckley would be able to drop the supplies precisely. This time the withering fire was too much; the DH-4 was brought down, killing Goettler instantly; Bleckley died of his wounds shortly thereafter. Both men were awarded the Medal of Honor.

Two other de Havilland crewmen also won the Medal of Honor. Second Lieutenant Ralph Talbot and Gunnery Sergeant Robert Guy Robinson of the First Marine Aviation Force were conducting a raid on October 14, 1918. Twelve enemy aircraft attacked and Gunnery Sergeant Robinson downed one, bringing his victory total to two. Robinson was hit by a bullet in his left arm, but carried on fighting until he collapsed from two more wounds, one in his stomach and one in his hip. His pilot, Lt. Talbot, had been equally aggressive shooting down one plane after Sgt. Robinson's collapse. Talbot finally dove away from the fight, crossed the lines at 50 feet altitude, and landed at the nearest field hospital so that Robinson could be treated.

Talbot and Robinson's exploit was one of many conducted by a neglected component of the U.S. World War I aviation effort. The U.S. Navy's Northern Bombing Group had been set up to undertake the destruction of the German submarine bases at Ostend, Zeebrugge, and Bruges and was to have one day wing and one night wing of six squadrons of bombers each. Problems in aircraft availability, personnel shortages, and some political questions involving the location of the bases forced a reduction in this strength to a total of eight squadrons.

The night bombing squadrons went through a frustrating sequence of events during which the Italian made Caproni bombers, which had been selected for equipment, were both slow in being delivered, and were equipped with Fiat engines of dubious reliability. Subsequently, a decision

The 2nd Aviation Instruction Center, Tours, October 9, 1918. (Peter M. Bowers Collection)

Winter in France. Note how Lewis guns have a jacket for protection. (Peter M. Bowers Collection)

Believed to be Issoudun, France; possibly Romorantin. (Peter M. Bowers Collection)

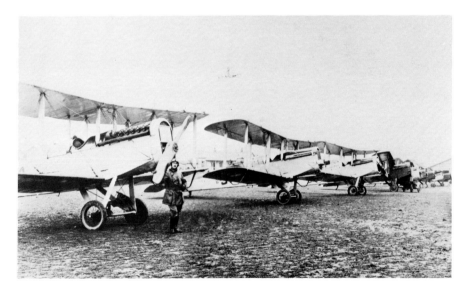

was made to equip with Handley Page bombers, but the war was over before these could begin operations.

The Marine Corps day bomber squadrons were to be equipped with American-built DH-4s, with the first aircraft arriving on September 7, 1918. Prior to its arrival, with a typical display of American enthusiasm, the Navy had persuaded the British to trade 54 de Havilland D.H.9s for Liberty engines, so that training and operations could begin.

The DH-4 was easily transported on a standard truck. (Peter M. Bowers Collection)

Scenes like this led to graphic descriptions of "billion dollar bonfires." Actually, good economic sense was used to determine whether or not the aircraft would be shipped home, and many were. (Peter M. Bowers Collection)

Typically for the times, the DH-4s that arrived were not really suitable for combat, and considerable tuning and refitting had to be done. Eager to engage, as always, the Marines began operations by transferring three observers and three pilots to Number 218 Squadron, RAF, to gain combat experience. Later a similar team was transferred to 217 Squadron. These flyers would participate in three raids each for experience before transferring back to the Northern Bombing Group.

As DH-4s began to arrive, U.S. crews in U.S. aircraft participated in raids with the 217 and 218 Squadrons to further the process of gaining experience. By October 14, 1918, sufficient aircraft had been mustered to carry out a raid on the railway facilities at Thielt by a mixed bag of DH-4s and D.H.9As of Number 9 squadron. Eight raids by Number 8 and 9 Squadrons were made in the next two weeks against a variety of transportation targets.

As tentative as the efforts might appear, the Northern Bombing Group was responsible for almost 78 tons of bombs being dropped on the retreating German forces. Perhaps more important, it established standards of enthusiasm, initiative, daring, and innovation for Naval and Marine air forces for the future.

Most of the work carried on by the DH-4 units was neither so dramatic nor so well reported as these two encounters, but it was often equally dangerous.

For most others, the war was less glorious, if not less hazardous. The St. Mihiel offensive provided the first opportunity for large-scale operations. The 1st Day Bombardment Group was formed two days before the offensive opened on September 11, and was composed of the 11th, 20th, and 96th Squadrons. The first two were equipped with Liberty planes, and the third with the favored French Breguet 14B-2.

The 1st Day Bombardment Group was directed to bomb hostile troop concentrations directly behind enemy lines. Weather was abominable, and they were forced to run the gauntlet of heavy fire from rifles, machine guns, and anti-aircraft artillery. The flying fields from which they operated were soaked with water and at one field fully 50% of the aircraft taking off had their propellers broken by mud thrown up from the wheels. Mud guards were promptly fabricated and installed, adding their mite to the already considerable weight and drag of the overloaded DH-4s.

The bombers became the primary target of the air opposition, particularly when weather, mechanical failures, and losses reduced formations to six or fewer aircraft. The 11th Squadron, which had not even completed its organization when committed to battle, lost five of six DH-4s on a single mission on September 18. It was serious schooling.

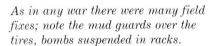

As in any war there were many field fixes; note the mud guards over the tires, bombs suspended in racks.

On September 16, six aircraft of the 20th Aero Squadron took off from Maulay to bomb the railroad yards at Longuyon. Five aircraft were forced to turn back due to engine troubles but the sixth, piloted by 1st Lt. Cecil G. Sellers, with Lt. Karl C. Payne as observer, pressed on. They were attacked by three of the formidable Fokker D VIIs on the way in and four more on returning, but they managed to drive them all off. Both officers received the Distinguished Service Cross for their heroism, which included putting the bombs squarely on target and probably shooting down one of the opposing Fokkers.

The 20th Squadron would not do so well eight days later. On September 26, the opening date of the Meuse-Argonne offensive, 10 aircraft, divided into two flights of five each, departed Maulay for a bombing raid on Dun-sur-Meuse, the ninth target that the Squadron had attacked since commencing operations. The raid went off well, but when crossing the lines on the return journey, all five aircraft of the second flight were shot down. Six men were killed and four taken prisoner. An observer in one of the returning aircraft was brought back dead.

Crash scenes; one can see how the legend arose that any landing you could walk away from was a good landing. Some of these were obviously not good landings.

Among the prisoners was 1st Lt. Merian C. Cooper, who would become a famous film producer; another was Guy Brown Wiser, who would have a successful career as an artist. Wiser, who died in 1983 at age 87, was the pilot and Lt. Glenn Richardson the observer in a DH-4 attacked by Lt. Alfred Greven in a Fokker D VII. Greven saw Richardson attempting to clear a jam and attacked. Richardson ripped off the drums of the Lewis guns and threw them at the Fokker in frustration, but Greven fired, hitting the reserve tank in the upper wing and the engine. The battle had begun at 14,000 feet, and Wiser glided down to a safe landing on a German airfield. There followed the customary photo session and a friendly luncheon before the two Americans were driven off to a captivity that ended on December 11, 1918.

The American squadrons learned quickly; during the Meuse-Argonne offensive, the units were flying in groups of 16 to 18 and these proved far less vulnerable to the rapidly tiring Germans. Raids were almost continuous, but the endless rhythm of bombing up, flying, dropping bombs and returning was highlighted by major successes. On September 29, the bombers hit railroad tracks and munition dumps at Grandpré and Marcq. On October 4, 3,000 pounds of bombs were delivered to Dun-sur-Meuse and Landres St. Georges. These were followed by similar achievements on October 18 and November 4. The war ended on November 11, just as the American units were beginning to hit their stride; the end was welcome nonetheless. The DH-4 had been successful, but it had shortcomings that were not easy to rectify and that loomed large when the aircraft was compared to its French competitors. The following is a famous analysis of the DH-4 and the Breguet 14 made in the Gorrell History of the Air Service, AEF:

"WHY THE DEHAVILLAND LIBERTY FOUR IS A POOR AIRPLANE FOR DAY BOMBARDMENT:

1. It is not fast at great altitudes with a load of bombs.

2. For a bombing plane it carries to any altitude an inferior quantity of bombs.

The USD-9A, the aircraft developed by the Engineering Division as a follow-on to the DH-4. It was a good airplane, but was too different in detail to fit into mass production easily, and the DH-4B was substituted.

3. The fuel tank between the pilot and observer is the target of every pursuit plane that attacks it.

4. The fuel tank is unsupported, works by pressure, and explodes when shot up.

5. When a bad landing is made or the plane crashes the tank leaves its bedding having nothing to keep it there, and crushes the pilot against the motor.

6. The pilot and observer are too far apart. Team work is necessary in a bombing plane, and it is impossible in this type. Speaking tubes help some but are not the remedy for this situation.

7. The observer's cockpit is too low and the seat belts provided are useless for active fighting. Any observer finds great difficulty in swinging twin Lewis guns in the blast of a Liberty tractor.

8. The controls are exposed and liable to be shot away by even a careful and conservative observer.

9. The arrangements for the throttle and switch are badly placed. They should be on the same side, thus making it unnecessary for the pilot to change his hands on the stick while landing.

10. The engine bed is weak.

11. The tail is weak and must be braced. Bracing is never as reliable as substantial construction.

12. The king posts on the elevators are weak and no wires (on the white ships) run from the king post to the trailing edge of the elevator.

13. The plane is blind from the pilot's and observer's standpoint.

14. The Liberty motor is too heavy and powerful for the DH-4. Anyone who has flown one can tell this by the vibration of the machine under full power.

15. The rubber connection to the gasoline line running parallel to the exhaust becomes heated and so works loose. This causes a flood of gasoline over the exhaust and resultant plane burned in the air. Have seen this happen on the ground.

16. The undercarriage is weak. In a crash there is a tendency for the motor to leave the plane: have witnessed at least one death as a result of this.

17. The plane is not so constructed that a bombing site can be used through the floor of the fuselage. This applies to carrying a large camera as well. It is possible, but not practical.

18. The gravity tank placed in the wings is not necessary and is dangerous.

19. The all-wood construction of the fuselage and wings tends to loosen more easily than would metal construction. The metal construction is used by both the French and Germans and had been found practical.

20. The bomb racks are not dependable, nor are capable of carrying large bombs. If small bombs are used, only a small number can be accommodated by the present bomb racks.

21. On the Liberty motor, the position of the spark plugs on the inside of the cylinders makes it necessary to wait for the engine to cool before changing the plugs. This means that a plane starting on a raid and finding a plug missing cannot get away on the raid. If the plugs were differently situated the plane could return to the field, change the plug, and still catch the formation."

"WHY THE FRENCH BREGUET BOMBER IS A SUCCESSFUL DAY BOMBING PLANE:

1. It is fast at high altitudes, on account of the large wing surface and will carry three times the load of a DH-4 to a higher altitude. Have been to

6,000 meters with 12 Michelin 90 kg bombs.

2. The Breguet squadrons can operate regulary at an ordinary altitude of 10,000 feet with 600 pounds of bombs, an armored seat for the pilot, twin Lewis guns, 6 drums of ammunition and the regulation front gun and ammunition.

3. The fuel system is divided into two tanks, the lower of which can be easily dropped in case of fire, and the upper so protected that it is very rarely set on fire.

4. Pilot and observer are close together so that conversation is easily carried on between them.

5. The observer's cockpit is deep so that the guns are easily swung and the observer requires no belt.

6. No controls are exposed.

7. The throttle arrangements are conveniently situated and excellent for the pilot.

8. The engine bed is strong. In our experience we have never seen the engine leave its bed in a Breguet crash.

9. The metal fuselage is strong so that the plane does not get out of line easily. Have seen a longeron entirely shot away and the plane return safely.

10. Both the pilot and observer have good visibility, enabling good formation work and protection.

11. The entire floor of the fuselage can easily be opened, thus giving an excellent visibility below and making practical an accurate bombsight.

12. The Michelin bomb racks are adjustable to any size bomb and still carry a full capacity load.

13. The struts cannot be shot apart by an explosive bullet.

14. From a standpoint of construction no stronger ship has probably ever been subjected to hard active service and given such excellent results.

15. We believe it possible to install a Liberty engine in a specially designed BREGUET and, as a result, have a plane close to the ideal bombing plane.

16. The present Renault BREGUET carries 5 hours fuel in addition to its capacity of bombs.

17. At a high altitude, it is just as easy to fly as a DH, since no stalling is necessary to hold the altitude once gained."

This analysis was perhaps unfair for the Breguet had some drawbacks, too.

The DH-4 was much better liked as an observation plane, for, unencumbered by a load of bombs, it flew high and fast. The observation work it did was invaluable, although the new American forces had to learn much in a hurry. They trained with French and British forces but, as in any practical endeavor, they learned at the front.

Corps Observation was dedicated to the needs of the Army for visual and photographic reconnaissance and for the adjustment of artillery fire. It was aided—or hampered, depending upon the maintenance—by modern equipment including radios and cameras, and the associated ground equipment necessary to use the results obtained from this equipment.

A wide variety of aircraft had been used for the initial operational work, everything from A.R.s, Sopwith 1½ Strutters, Spad XIs and XVIs, Breguets, Salmsons, and even F.E. 2bs.

Army Observation did not get a start until September 16, with the formation of the first Army Observation Group. Duties were essentially similar to the Corps Observation, but the reporting was more immediate. Training had not been as intensive as that received by the Corps Observation crews, and there were many of the ordinary vicissitudes of war; for example, they had received photographic plates from the French that proved to have been exposed to the light, rendering many hazardous missions useless.

Army Observation came into its own, as did its bombing counterpart, during the St. Mihiel offensive. Each day, prior to the next day's attack, artillery objectives were photographed and complete visual and photographic reconnaissance was made of the enemy's lines of communication and billeting areas. During the attack, observation planes were maintained "in a continuous barrage" over enemy lines, watching out for enemy movements, particularly reinforcements.

Formations of three aircraft at a time left the aerodromes, as they were then called, at intervals of two hours. Often DH-4s were assigned as protection flights (top cover) for other DH-4s doing photographic work or artillery registration. During the latter work at least one incident occurred when a DH-4 of the 135th Aero Squadron was blown up in flight by a passing artillery shell.

Just as with the bombing forces, the observation units were just beginning to acquire a genuine proficiency when the war ended. All of the myriad tasks of training, supply, and coordination with the other branches had just been learned; personnel were becoming comfortable with their machines and their mission; and the DH-4 itself was at last having the bugs worked out of it. The work done until November 11th was skillful and courageous, but it was obviously fundamental preparation for a much greater effort in 1919, which providentially was not needed.

Postwar Use

The end of a war is usually the end of the road for most warplanes; for the DH-4 it was a new beginning. The U.S. Army Air Service had already decided upon a program that would remove most of the operational drawbacks from the aircraft, creating the DH-4B that interchanged the location of the fuel tank and the front cockpit. Over 1,500 "Liberty Planes" were treated to this conversion between 1919 and 1923. The principal structural change, apart from the cockpit relocation, was the "planking" of the entire fuselage length with plywood for additional strength.

In the conversion process there was a whole series of subtypes developed and many special-purpose aircraft fitted out for a specific test, flight or experiment. In tactical terms, the DH-4 was perfectly adequate as it was; there was no war going on, so there was no enemy opposition. It could still be used for practice gunnery, bombing, and other purposes, and what was undoubtedly tight-fisted penny pinching on the part of Congress was no genuine drawback to the actual needs of the service.

One endearing feature of the DH-4 that made this so was its absolutely straightforward flying characteristics. Major General Leigh Wade, USAF (Retired), pilot of one of the "Round the World" Douglas World Cruisers, flew the DH-4s in France as a test pilot, and subsequently in his routine service experience. He recalls that it was an ordinary airplane that flew exactly as he expected it to, with no unreasonable virtues, nor unconscionable vices. Having flown many planes of the same size and power rating, he stepped into the DH-4 in France without any difficulty and, in fact, recalls only one DH-4 flight in particular. He was flying from Dayton to Washington D.C. in a DH-4 with the famous airman, Jimmy Doolittle, as his pilot. Wade was in the back seat, writing a letter to his mother and one to his sweet-

The Museum's DH-4 suspended in the Arts and Industries building. Note absence of insignia; this has not been satisfactorily explained. The photograph is a perfect example of old style Museum technique in terms of cases and displays.

The Museum's aircraft after being
"refurbished" by Dayton-Wright, prior
to shipment to the Museum.

On exhibit in the "old tin shed" that for years served as the National Air Museum. Billy Mitchell's Spad XVI in background is now on display at NASM; Curtiss flying boat at right has only hull remaining.

heart; after a while he simply went to sleep. When they landed, Doolittle asked him how he liked the violent weather over the Alleghenies; Wade honestly replied that he had slept through it. Doolittle didn't believe him and later always kidded Wade about trying to one-up him with his "nervelessness." But this is not why Wade remembers the flight; he recalls the flight because he inadvertently put his sweetheart's letter in the envelope to his mother and vice versa. The sweetheart was very understanding, but the mother was somewhat upset.

Lt. Gen. Laurence C. Craigie, USAF (Retired), also flew the DH-4 extensively, beginning as a student. Craigie had trained at Brookley Field during 1923 and 1924, flying first Jennies, then the DH-4, before going on to S.E.5s and Boeing MB-3As. During his later days on the DH-4 he did his bit for the modernization program by pranging two DH-4Bs in five days. Craigie recalls that the DH-4 was pleasant to fly, a "good honest flying machine," especially valued because it had decent ground handling characteristics, a rarity at the time. The Liberty engine was regarded as reliable— all things are relative—although forced landings were routine. Anything short of flying straight into a brick wall could be walked away from, particularly if the pilot had enough control remaining to stick the wing into the ground and let the general collapse of wood, fabric and wires absorb the

Above right: A post-war photo of a DH-4B, with the improved seating position and other modifications.

Right: A USMC DH-4B from the U.S. Naval Aircraft Factory.

The DH-4 Amb-2 converted ambulance plane. It was a pretty clever adaptation.

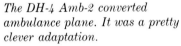

shock. The DH-4Bs with their wooden fuselage were more hazardous in a crash than the later DH-4Ms, which had steel tube fuselage construction, but the latter were heavier and less pleasant to fly.

In May of 1925, Craigie was instructing in the Advanced Flying School at Kelly Field and was asked to fly a Sergeant up to Waco, Texas, about 200 miles north, because the Sergeant's wife was seriously ill there. He gladly agreed and in short order (about two hours later) they were circling Waco, looking for a landing spot as near as possible to the Sergeant's wife's house. Craigie dragged a field, made a nice landing, and saw the Sergeant off on his mission of mercy. Craigie taxied back to the end of the field and gave the Liberty the gun for take-off. The field had been planted in cotton and the rows gave the airplane a rather bumpy take-off, so bumpy that the carburetor float on the Liberty engine lifted off its seat, resulting in momentary fuel stoppages.

The carburetor burped often enough to appreciably lengthen the take-off

68

One of an endless string of modifications the DH-4 was "treated" to. This one has hydrovanes and flotation bags. Note McCook Field number P-175.

run—in fact it lengthened it to the point that a hedge at the edge of the field caught the landing gear spreader bar, causing Craigie to veer straight towards a house, hovering just above a stall, chunks of hedge still clinging to the spreader bar, engine still running intermittently. Craigie saw that he wasn't going to fly, wasn't going to the clear the house, and was about to run out of ideas. He instinctively slipped the plane and the left wing stuck in the ground, cartwheeling it into the front yard of the house and, incidentally, knocking off a corner of the residence. The DH-4 was upside down, a notoriously bad position to be in because of the danger of fire from fuel dripping on the hot engine. Craigie unbuckled his seat belt, dropped out and escaped none the worse for wear except for a slight bruise on the leg. An elderly lady was occupying the front corner of the house, under doctor's orders to avoid any sudden shock as she was recovering from a heart attack. Fortunately it didn't bother her at all; she seemed rather to enjoy it, Craigie recalls. At the time, he thought "Oh well, it is all in a good cause."

A silver doped DH-4B built by the Gallaudet Company. (Peter M. Bowers Collection)

Above right: A whole series of ski types were developed for the DH-4. (Peter M. Bowers Collection)

A DH-4B was fitted with a geared, supercharged engine and a larger diameter, 4-blade propeller, for high altitude work. The extended landing gear provided a higher altitude right on the ground. (Peter M. Bowers Collection)

One of several modifications to the basic design to provide an enclosed canopy. This was produced for civil use; the aircraft was still not able to excite much interest as a practical business machine. (Peter M. Bowers Collection)

A week later, he was sent back to pick up the Sergeant. On his take off from Waco, the Liberty failed, and he wound up in a ditch, the airplane O.K. except for cracked engine mounts. Craigie is probably still the world's record holder for the most DH-4s cracked up on the outskirts of Waco, Texas, in one week. As an interesting side note, it developed that the lady the Sergeant was visiting was neither ill nor his wife. But it was still in a good cause.

The number one Boeing XDH-4M, built with a metal fuselage. (Peter M. Bowers Collection)

Some of the modifications became extreme; this is a "deep belly" modified mail plane. (Peter M. Bowers Collection)

Bellanca wings and lifting struts were fitted to some DH-4 fuselages to create a new mail plane. (Peter M. Bowers Collection)

This is the standard DH-4 mail plane conversion, with long exhaust pipe to avoid blinding pilot at night with exhaust flames and landing lights built into upper wing. Exhaust pipe was later deleted as it proved a fire hazard in the event of a crash. (Peter M. Bowers Collection)

Yet another version of an enclosed cockpit; often called the "Honeymoon Express."

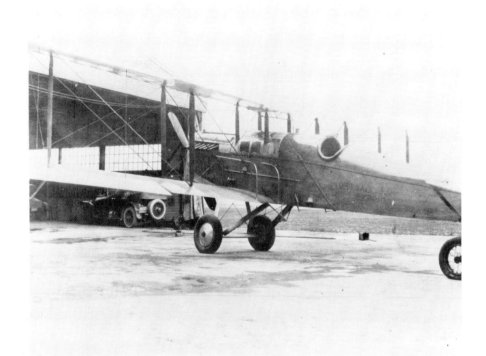

The postwar DH-4s were used in a bewildering variety of record flights, the most demanding being the wonderful transcontinental reliability contest of 1919, and the New York to Alaska flight of 1920. Both were major accomplishments, using the technology that had almost literally been conjured up overnight.

The DH-4 was flown by every major figure in U.S. military aviation, including the inimitable Jimmy Doolittle. First Lieutenant Doolittle made a record-breaking transcontinental flight in 21 hours and 20 minutes during September 4-5, 1922. His DH-4B was extensively modified for the flight. Considerable extra wire bracing was required to provide the structural strength required for the 240 gallon fuel tank, and plywood covering was added wherever there were known or suspected structural weaknesses. The older DH-4 ash landing gear was used because it was four inches higher and provided more clearance for the larger Martin propeller that was installed for extra range. A supplementary wing, 17 inches wide and 48 inches long was placed on the landing gear, ala Fokker practice, for a little extra lift. Special wings of selected spruce were built to obtain the greatest strength with lightest weight. Even when fully loaded, Doolittle's modified de Havilland took off in 350 yards and cruised at about 105 mph. As a satisfactory commercial note, Doolittle wrote later that "Penzoil (sic) Triple Heavy oil was used throughout the trip and found very satisfactory."

Lt. Harold R. Harris, later a Brigadier General and a brilliant leader in commercial aviation, used a supercharged DH-4B to reach an altitude of 27,000 feet, higher than Geoffrey de Havilland had ever contemplated for his product.

Perhaps a more portentous event occurred on June 25, 1923, when Lts. Lowell Smith and Paul Richter achieved the first in-flight refueling in DH-4Bs, over San Diego. Smith and Richter later made an endurance flight of 36 hours and 15 minutes on August 27-28, in the process setting a number of weight and distance records. In October they made a non-stop flight from

Colonel Billy Mitchell had a specially cleaned up DH-4B for his personal use. Note his insignia under cockpit.

The de Havilland D.H.9a was not a
success; it had a better airframe, but
a far inferior engine.

The Salmson A-2 was a rugged
aircraft with fair performance, well
liked by its pilots. Engine was a
radial, watercooled type, most
unusual.

The angular Breguet 14 was preferred by many pilots.

the Canadian Border to Mexico in their in-flight refueled DH-4B.

There were no less that 23 official varieties of DH-4Bs by March 16, 1925, ranging from the standard DH-4B to the XDH-4B5, used for "an experimental airways airplane built in accordance with the Engineering Division's drawings for carrying passengers or freight."[7]

Surplused DH-4s and DH-4Bs appeared in civil guise, working as mailplanes, where they were much modified, and as Forest Fire Patrol planes. Some were used in films and many were acquired by private companies for a variety of purposes.

The Steel Tube DH-4M

The DH-4B had solved many of the "flaming coffin" problems, but the wooden fuselage construction left a lot to be desired in the event of a crash. Brigadier General William Mitchell had made a whirlwind European tour in 1922, and he was vastly impressed by the use of welded steel tube fuselage in

Interesting shot of DH-4 with air and ground crew posed. Note rocks with rope attached used for chocks.

Every conceivable type of test was run with DH-4s; this is a 37 mm Baldwin cannon being tested.

*Captain Harold R. Harris at right by
a DH-4 cleaned up for racing.*

the Fokker aircraft he saw. In a budgeting ploy as old as the military services, Mitchell had maintenance funds used to build new fuselages of steel tubing for DH-4 wings, empennages, and equipment. The Boeing Company was sustained by an order for 180 DH-4M-1s while Tony Fokker's American venture, the Atlantic Aircraft Corporation, built 135 DH-4M-2s.

The DH-4Ms were safer but heavier, and they labored on in the Army until 1932, when the last four were retired.

It would be impossible to recount all of the modifications made to all of the DH-4s, but in January, 1924, G.W. Carr, an engineer at McCook Field, made an attempt in the excellent magazine, *U.S. Air Services*. In his summary, he notes that the principal changes for the DH-4B included moving the fuel tank forward, moving the cockpit to the rear with the necessary changes in controls, and redesigning the instrument board. One hundred and fifty of these DH-4Bs were constructed by the L.W.F. Engineering Company, 50 by Aeromarine Plane & Motor Corporation, and 50 by the Gallaudet Aircraft Corporation.

In 1921 the Engineering Division of McCook Field specified an additional twelve modifications. These were:

First. The fuel system was changed from an engine-driven air-pressure system with an auxiliary pump in the pilot's cockpit to an engine-driven bellows-pump system that entirely eliminated the air pressure, and with it the primary cause of the "Flaming Coffin" appellation.

Second. A centrifugal booster pump was installed in the pilot's cockpit. This pump enabled the pilot to fill the gravity tank from the main tank should any trouble be experienced with the pumping system. The pump could then be cut out and the engine operated from gravity.

Third. The plain DH-4 fuel tanks, both main and gravity, were replaced by leakproof rubber-covered tanks. These tanks were not only leakproof but were crashproof, which further lessened the fire hazard in event of crash.

Fourth. New type landing gear struts were installed and the landing gear axle moved forward 7½ inches.

Fifth. A new type of seat was installed.

Sixth. The 750 by 125 millimeter wheels were replaced by the Handley-Page 900 by 200 millimeter wheel, which was considerably stronger and made the airplane easier to handle in landing.

Seventh. The service had been urging for some time that provision be made to carry an extra wheel as replacement in case of damage. A spare-wheel carrier was therefore installed, permitting an extra wheel to be carried under the fuselage.

Eighth. The CC Gun Synchronizer used during the war was superseded by the Nelson Gun Control Synchronizer and the Marlin machine guns were moved slightly to the rear.

Ninth. Better cooling was provided by the installation of a longer radiator with long-type shutters.

Tenth. The Delco Buzzer Starter System was installed.

Eleventh. A double-ignition battery was installed, making it possible to go on long-distance flights without the fear of the single battery running out.

Twelfth. The instrument board was again revised and the compass was removed entirely from the cockpit and placed in the upper center section. The inverted-type compass was used in this installation.

Two hundred DH-4Bs were modified accordingly, 50 each by the Boeing Airplane Company, the Wittemann Aircraft Corporation, Aeromarine, and Thomas-Morse Aircraft Corporation.

Left: A typical post-war scene. These are DH-4Bs of the 99th Aero Squadron at Shepards Airway Landing Field, Martinsburg, West Virginia, April 9, 1925.

In late 1922 five further equipment modifications were authorized, as follows:

First. The inverted-type compass in the upper center section was replaced by the standard compass again mounted on the instrument board.

Second. A bank and turn indicator, a newly developed instrument, was added to the instrument board.

Third. Provision was made for the installation of up-to-date bombing equipment utilizing the Type L-1 Bomb Release Handle and the Type A-2 Bomb Rack. This was the dual control installation and could be operated from either cockpit.

Fourth. Provision was made for the installation of the newly developed SCR 134 Radio Telephone Set, which in turn required the installation of the AS-2 Storage Battery.

Fifth. The tail skid box was reinforced to prevent failure in hard landings.

More important, however, General Mitchell's desire for steel tube fuselage aircraft was finally brought to reality with contracts to build the DH-4M-1. The main change was, of course, the steel tube fuselage, but an additional nine changes were made:

First. An entirely new fuel system was provided, eliminating the main fuel tank from the fuselage, providing for wing tanks, and using the engine-driven gear pump instead of the Sylphon pump previously employed.

Second. A new 14-gallon oil tank was installed.

Third. The clincher-type tire that had been used on the 900 by 200 Palmer Type Wheel had been obsolete for some time, but due to the quantities available in Air Service stores DH-4B airplanes had continued to use them. The stock of these wheels, tires and tubes had been reduced to a point where it was deemed advisable to adopt the 36 by 8 straight-side equipment. These were called for on the DH-4M-1.

Fourth. The K-1 Camera was replaced by the K-3.

Fifth. The space that had been occupied by the main fuel tank was converted into a baggage compartment, which was undoubtedly of great value in cross-country flying.

Sixth. The two 30-caliber Marlin machine guns were replaced by one 30-caliber Browning machine gun.

Seventh. The change in the airplane made it possible to utilize a new instrument board of simpler construction.

Eighth. The standard compass was removed from the instrument board and moved to the cowling above and slightly forward of the instrument board.

Ninth. A water-line strainer was installed.

Boeing built 150 DH-4M-1s, while Aeromarine built 135 DH-4M-2s.

In addition to these prescribed, "government issue" changes, there were many experiments intended to improve the overall performance of the airplane. Boeing built new wings, using Goettingen 436 airfoils, and a modified empennage, calling the rather handsome result the XCO-7; the performance was mildly better, but hardly worth the expense of the new type.

In a similar way, thicker wings with a Bellanca lifting strut were tried on an otherwise stock DH-4B; there was no significant improvement.

The DH-4 served a host of users including the U.S. Navy, Marine Corps, Post Office, Forest Service, and some private owners. The Post Office had received about 100 DH-4s for the Air Mail Service, operating them at first

*Parachutists dropping from formation
of DH-4M2s, built by Atlantic
Aircraft Corporation (Fokker).*

*The twin engine DH-4 was not
successful; problems were multiplied
while reliability dropped.*

A DH-4B built by the Aeromarine Company, at Wichita, Labor Day, 1924. (Walter House Collection)

Lt. W.D. Coney beside the aircraft he used in a trans-continental attempt in February, 1921.

Top: "Instruction in starting the motor, Crissy Field, California, June/July, 1923, Air Service ROTC Camp."

Bottom: Lt. Lowell Smith and Lt. Paul Richter demonstrated the practicability of in-flight refueling with the DH-4 in 1923.

Typical post-World War I scene—a DH-4 of the 90th Squadron, Sanderson, Texas.

between New York and Chicago. Thirty of the DH-4s were modified to a twin-engine configuration; the attempt was a failure. From July 1, 1921 until 1926, the DH-4 was standard equipment, carrying as much as 550 pounds of mail over the segments that made up a 2,680 mile transcontinental system. It was truly a time of iron men in wooden aircraft.

The attraction of the DH-4 was primarily that it was available to government agencies at almost no outlay costs. Maintenance and operating costs were something else, of course, and by 1924 and 1925 the attrition of DH-4s was such that they began to disappear from use.

The Air Service used them, as the long list of types indicates, for every conceivable purpose, including an amazing variety of experiments with superchargers, controllable pitch propellers, reversible propellers, parachute operations, in-flight refueling, VIP transports, engine test beds, armament tests, crash tests, fire tests, streamlining tests and, improbable as it may seem, for racing.

In this long process there emerged a utility aircraft eminently suited to the times. Other countries, notably France, were more dynamic in their development of new types, and more consistently introduced these into service. And yet, these new types were not remarkably different in performance, dependability, or configuration than the proven DH-4. European countries with empires perhaps needed to continue the development effort at a slightly more accelerated pace than America but for all practical purposes the slender winged, narrow fuselaged creation of de Havilland was adequate to the needs.

By this time, the DH-4 had long passed its potential as an airframe; it was simply a serving maiden, tractable, inexpensive, relatively safe to operate, and, until the mid 1920s, always available. It was enough to sustain not only the Air Service, but a dozen other users until the economy and technology had forced a change. As such, it had achieved a second career that was far more important than that originally intended for it.

Restoring the Museum's Aircraft

ompared to typical restorations at the Garber Facility, the DH-4 was, in an appropriate RAF term, a "piece of cake." The entire aircraft was available—no hard-to-find missing parts—and it was in relatively good shape for a 62-year veteran of an intensive flight test program and years of exhibit and long term storage.

The first of all of the American DH-4s was unique in many ways. As noted previously, it had been built with incredible speed by a dedicated team at Dayton-Wright, using just converted English drawings and a sample DH-4, sans engine, as an example. Consequently, it had a number of features not found in production aircraft, Dayton-Wright having, with unusual foresight for the period, decided to use the *thirtieth* example from their line as the

Karl Heinzel working on the No. 4 Liberty engine. The engine was started first, as a method of easing into the project.

Distributor disassembled shows degree of care with which restoration is done; Liberty engines were unusual in having a battery system rather than a magneto system for ignition.

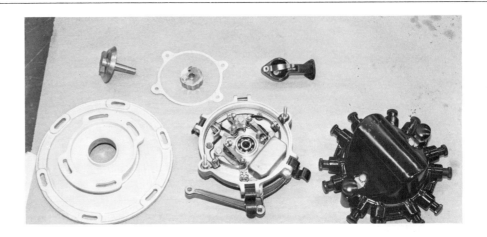

production standard. The original American DH-4, "Old Yellow," differed in having a radiator overhead surge tank placed in the center section of the upper wing, with a long pipe connecting it to the top of the radiator. A 66-gallon fuel tank was installed in the fuselage; this was later changed in production to the standard 88-gallon size. The rear turtledeck, extending down from the aft cockpit, was a removable structure for some undetermined reason and there were numerous minor details that eventually differed on production airplanes.

One major difference, of course, was the color scheme, which on the first example can only be called "early haphazard." The fuselage was cream (hence the nickname "Old Yellow"), with a brown top surface. The wings and empennage were clear doped, with unpinked taping showing through. The rudder had the red, white and blue stripes neatly in reverse order to what

De-skinned and awaiting restoration.

became production standard and only two national insignia were applied, one familiar red-centered white star on a blue disc under each lower wing tip. As a final concession to the haste of the times, the starboard star was not centered properly, and when the aircraft was restored it was painted on cattywampus just as it had been originally.

The aircraft had a long service life of more than 1,078 flying hours in test and routine hack work, an incredible accumulation of time in a period when aircraft often lasted less than 100 hours due to the outdoor storage, appalling landing fields, and frequent forced landings and crashes. It was the second plane flown with the Liberty Twelve engine; the first had been a Navy Curtiss HS-1 flying boat; an LWF had flown earlier with the Liberty Eight. It made more than 4,000 flights, conducted 2,500 experiments (usually equipment modifications), traveled more than 111,000 miles, made 28 trips from Dayton to such distant spots as Philadelphia, New York, and Washington, and in general served like a distinguished end product of a long line of development rather than a "first shot prototype." One interesting side note is that both Orville Wright and Glenn L. Martin had flights in the aircraft. During its life a number of modifications were made. Additional wing ribs were placed in the slip stream of the propeller, and various repairs were made, including extensive work on the landing gear.

At the end of the war, when Dayton-Wright and all the other manufacturers had their vast production contracts either cancelled or curtailed, Colonel Sidney D. Waldon, of the U.S. Air Service, wrote on December 9, 1918, to Dr. Charles D. Walcott, Secretary of the Smithsonian, offering the "Original No. 1 DeHavilland Plane" for permanent exhibit. In his letter Waldon notes that all of the time flown by the airplane had been put on by Howard Rinehart, "one of the greatest pilots there is."

The letter coincided happily with an exhibit in Washington that the Army and the Smithsonian were planning and, after a quick check to see that

The fuselage was de-skinned, and cleaned. It was in remarkably good condition, and almost all the parts could be retained.

The disastrous location of the main fuel tank is evident here.

Rich Horigan repairing forward fuselage skinning.

Horigan assembling vertical surface.

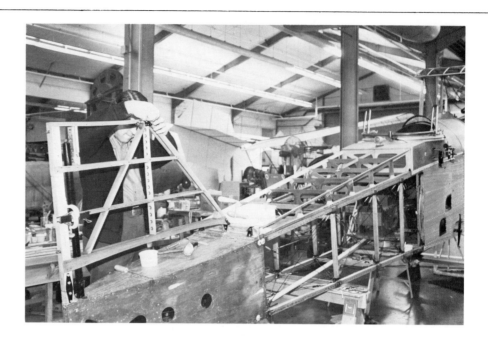

The cockpit before refurbishing.

everyone was in agreement that the DH-4 should be accepted and displayed, Secretary Walcott replied on December 19 that the Smithsonian Institution would be very glad to accept the aircraft.

The next bit of correspondence reveals that on January 27, 1919, the Army gave Dayton-Wright instructions to ship the aircraft to arrive at the Smithsonian Institution no later than March 15, 1919.

Dayton-Wright was overjoyed at the prospect of their prize being exhibited at the already venerable Smithsonian Institution, and Harold E. Talbott, Jr., wrote an enthusiastic letter of thanks to Walcott. He also authorized someone to "refurbish" the aircraft to combat standard. The original paint was superseded by the current military specification of olive drab overall, cocarde markings, and a complete panoply of military equipment including machine guns (two Marlin and two Lewis), gun mounts, gun sights, (two Lewis wind vanes, one Marlin Ring, one Marlin bead), Very pistol, generators, oxygen equipment, bombsight, heated flying suits, bomb racks and bombs, aerial reel, radio, etc. Finally, as an afterthought, a serial number was assigned: SC 29159, the 3,101 aircraft of a 4,000 aircraft contract. Apparently, and with good logic, someone decided that the previously unnumbered No. 1 prototype should receive a serial number and that it should be the next one that Dayton-Wright would have used. In a way it is perfectly fitting, for it reveals to the cognoscenti exactly how many DH-4s were built at Dayton-Wright.

Cockpit details.

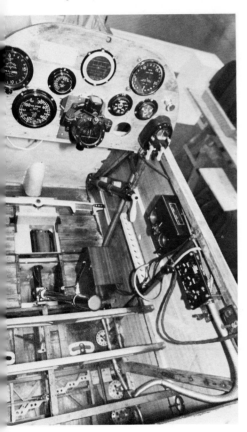

Top right: The instrument panel before refinishing.

Right: Technician working on leather coaming. Note Lexol in background, wonderful for leather products.

The aircraft was delivered with a later engine and propeller, while the "original" Liberty and propeller with which it had made the first flight were shipped separately. It should be noted that the "original" Liberty was in fact the fourth engine that Packard had built, but was the first DH-4 flight article.

Over the years the DH-4 endured the usual indignities suffered by aircraft in museums; it was repainted, had markings added and deleted, and then was placed in storage. At one point it was removed from storage for exhibit at Langley Air Force Base for an Armed Forces Day celebration; it was hastily patched up and repainted, apparently by someone brought up on all-metal aircraft, and then placed back in storage at the Garber Facility. Still, it had not suffered badly and was fair game to the talented team of Rich Horigan and Karl Heinzel who were given the task of restoring it, beginning on April 18, 1980.

Richard D. Horigan, Jr., is a veteran of many restorations, including the Albatros D Va and the Bellanca C.F., on which he worked with his partner, Karl Heinzel. They form a good team. Horigan is rather quiet, almost shy; Heinzel is a late-blooming product of the flower child generation, and gets understandably annoyed when we kid him about being our "hippy dippy" restorer. Both men are totally dedicated to their profession, and both work with great zeal and extraordinary skill.

The following account of the restoration is derived from tape recorded sessions with the two men, and is very largely in their own words. It is helpful to relate a restoration in this manner, for the challenges of restoration are not always the same as the challenges of design or manufacture. In discussing the general design of an aircraft it is necessary to deal with airfoils, horsepower, drag and factors affecting performance; in discussing a restoration it is more important to record the replacement of oil-soaked wood or the repair of a previously damaged landing gear, for these items make the greatest demand on the restorer's talents.

There are certain prerequisites to all restorations and these were done on the DH-4. It was carefully transported from storage, cleaned, and then further disassembled. A restoration package had already been prepared by

The work becomes intense as it progresses; note Horigan's concentration as he fits metal parts to completed cockpit coaming.

Radio component, complete with original wiring diagram.

Curator of Aircraft, Bob Mikesh, and photographs were taken of the disassembly process. Let's begin the actual restoration, as Rich and Karl did, with bits and pieces and then the engine.

Oddments and Engine

Horigan and Heinzel recount: "We actually started on the airplane while waiting for the dope and paint to dry on the Bellanca C.F. Karl and I started repairing the camera and various small pieces, but when we finally got on the airplane full-time, we took off the cowling and the radiator and removed the Liberty engine. We placed it on a stand that can be rotated so that we could work on it inverted, if necessary. We were fortunate to have the basic manual for the engine, which was invaluable.

"We took the sub-assemblies of the engine apart and cleaned them as units. We removed the wiring harness, then the valve train. At this point we determined that the water manifold could not be taken out as a unit until the jugs (cylinders) were removed, and it was necessary to remove them almost three at a time. The carburetors mount through the water jacket and were removed from underneath it. All accessories, like the magneto, generator, and so on, were removed.

"The engine was then turned over so that we could remove the bottom case and get to the rod bolts. After we removed all the pistons we broke the case apart and inspected the crankshaft, which was found to be in excellent condition. The engine was almost free from corrosion except for some pitting around the valve seats where the valves had been left in an open position.

"All of the items were chemically cleaned and then readied for reassembly. The piston rings had been removed, as the manual had suggested, by using three hacksaw blades with their edges filed off to slip into the rings and then lift them up off the piston.

"After the engine case had been assembled, we turned our attention to the cylinders. They were painted a basic army olive drab and were made out of

Two wind-driven generators, one for
the heated flying suits, and one for
the radio equipment.

The upper wing section contained a
radiator header tank; not a good
location in the event of leaks.

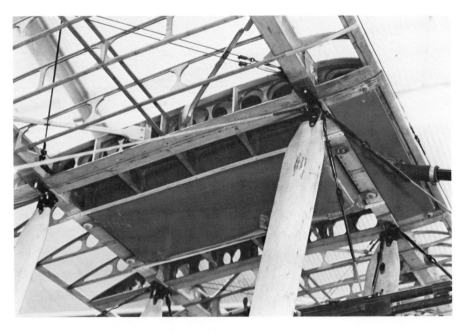

welded steel (one of the advanced features of the Liberty). We processed
them in the rust stripper, gave them a thorough washing, and then blasted
the exterior, capping them so that sand particles couldn't get inside. We then
gave them a phosphate coating, zinc chromated them, and painted them in
olive drab.

"The water jacket had been cleaned and preserved, then filled with soft
seal (a proprietary preserving compound) and jostled around before being
drained. There was very little pitting on the interior of the cylinder walls,
usually only where the valves had been positioned open. The cylinders were
given a heavy coating of grease, as were the pistons.

"In putting the cylinders on, it was necessary to remember to leave all the
bolts very loose, as the water manifold had to be placed on at the same time.
Once the manifolds were on, we re-installed the two Zenith carburetors (one

for each cylinder bank). These were in excellent condition, being made of cast aluminum with mostly brass fittings.

"This particular Liberty had a lot of nickel plate, used on the mag drive covers and all of the pushrods and carburetor linkage.

"We re-installed the fuel tank pressurizing air pump on the rear of the engine, which, curiously, also had the cam lobes fitted to it for the machine gun synchronization.

"And for the record, next to the right magneto drive there is a big number '4' stamped on the case.

"The exhaust stacks were found to have a gun-blue type finish; they had

Rich and Karl divided the work as they went along, but were of course always on hand to help each other.

The latest in tools: paperclipping wing ribs together. It works.

been cracked in numerous spots, and we first welded them and then reblued them, finishing off with a water white coat (a clear thin preservative) for protection. The exhaust stacks were interesting in that they had certain dents and dings which were pictured in contemporary photos, enabling us to further fix the identity of the aircraft.

"An interesting example of how the art of restoration tries to conceal itself behind the original item was the way we modified the original gaskets. These gaskets were used on the water jackets, the carburetor intake and on the exhaust ports. On the intake side they were of a paper material, while on the exhaust side they were composed of copper and asbestos. In between, we fashioned a thin paper gasket soaked in soft seal with a very small hole in the center, to relieve pressure if the engine was ever turned over. The soft seal keeps the hole closed and moisture out of the interior of the engine, but the installation appears perfectly standard."

Fuselage, Front to Rear
"When we received the plane from storage, all of the original wood was there except for three pieces of plywood from the firewall back on the right side of the aircraft. We removed the original plywood of the forward right side of the engine bay, and found to our surprise that no glue was used in the aircraft fuselage; everything—ply covering, bulkheads, longerons, etc.— was held together with wood screws and bolts. We removed the # 1, 2, and 3 bulkheads, which were in poor shape, being oil soaked, rotten, and damaged. We soaked them for three days in a mixture of 50% Varsol and 50% trichloro-ethylene, to suck out the oil. The bulkheads were then dried, repaired, refinished and put back into the airplane. The original plywood was returned to the exterior of the engine bay, and we repainted the interior in its original cream color, the same that is used on the exterior."

Cockpits
"We found the original brown color used for restoration underneath the gunmounts when we removed them. We took out the ammo boxes, instruments, seats and control sticks, throttles, gun triggers, etc. All the instru-

The finished product begins to take shape.

ments were taken apart, restored, and preserved. The manufacturer's name plate was also found, with the number 29159 on it.

"The floorboard was somewhat novel in that it was standard tongue and groove just like the flooring in houses used to be. The bomb release mechanism, made of stamped steel, finished blue, was located under the front floor boards. This was a relatively simple but effective cam mechanism which operated two push rods which in turn pickled the bomb release mechanism on the wing racks.

"The rest of the cockpit was in pretty good shape, except for the leather cockpit coaming headrest, belts and the seats. We salvaged as much as was possible by soaking the original material in Lexol and then reforming them to the original shapes. Karl suggests that 'nobody sit in the cockpit unless they are extremely dignified, as excessive bending of the leather will wreck the finish.' '

Between the two cockpits, in the position that made it the DH-4's bête noire, was the 66-gallon fuel tank. It was made of a galvanized steel material called Turnplate, and in one of the refreshing human touches of restoration, was found to have penciled on it the name of R. E. Maxwell, Dayton, Ohio, presumably a worker at Dayton-Wright. The fuel tank was stripped, chemically treated, repainted and well sloshed with soft seal before being drained. It was reinstalled along with its associated plumbing, cables, etc.

The most puzzling challenge in the cockpit area was the rear gun Scarff

There comes a time in every assembly process when Joe Fichera and his big hammer are called for.

ring, where it was difficult to determine how to install the bearings in the sealed ring unit. Rich finally figured that the bearings must have been placed inside the ring in heavy grease, and then a magnet was used to get the bearing studs into place.

The restoration team resumes: "We tackled the rear fuselage next, where each of the four longerons connected to the forward fuselage by two flat steel plates and six bolts. This facilitated both shipment overseas and repair in the field. Removing the fuselage made reinstallation of the camera, radios, instruments and top covers to the rest of the cockpit easy. New plywood was applied to the right side of the fuselage and footsteps were installed, based on the photographs of the plane.

"The four main longerons are, of course, braced by horizontal and vertical members, which are themselves wire braced. These members are not actually attached to the longerons, but are wire braced to sit in cups on either side. All of the metal fittings in the aircraft, and there were thousands, were painted black, including the bracing wires. The longerons were in excellent condition, still with original wrapping on beneath the cups, and were merely cleaned with acetone and revarnished. Some of the exterior plywood of the rear fuselage had delaminated and we would take a jackknife blade, open up

The airplane is assembled before recovering to check fits, rigging, etc.

All work and no play would make Karl a dull boy. Karl is not dull.

the delaminations as much as possible, and smear epoxy glue inside. Then we'd clamp flat pieces of wood on each side, sand it and refinish it.

"The rear of the fuselage was, of course, smaller diameter and quite crowded with the elaborate tail skid mechanism and the stablizer trim adjustment. The stabilizer was mounted to a bar that rides up and down and is adjusted from the front cockpit via cables and worm gear.

"The turtledeck had originally been made to be removable and was held by four brass hinges on each side; later in the plane's service life, it was made non-removable.

"The belly of the fuselage was plywood that had been replaced sometime after 1957, probably at Langley, and this was all removed and replaced.

"The fuselage was now substantially complete, and we turned our attention to the landing gear, which had naturally and obviously received the worst treatment in its 4,000 landings.

"The landing gear, large angled vee sections of spruce, had been broken on the right side. When it was repaired, there had been no effort to replace the wood; instead, steel plates had been screwed onto it for reinforcement. The left side had also been damaged, and all four spruce plates which fitted the four legs of the landing gear had to be replaced. The gear had some shock absorbing quality due to the four bungee cords by which the axle was attached to the struts. The entire landing gear, including the spreader bar, required loving attention to repair all of the cracks, dings, and other damage.

"The Goodyear Tire and Rubber Company very generously made up two tires for the de Havilland, fitting them to the wheels and making them in a mold, just as if they planned on a production run.

"The airplane had a steerable tail skid installation that also showed evidence of hard use. The skid itself is made of a single piece of ash or oak, and is encased in steel that has lightening holes cut into it. This unit is mounted on a shaft that goes up into the fuselage into a socket; it has two heavy-duty springs on a bell crank arm that hook onto the rudder post. The springs acted as shock absorbers so that the rudder wasn't jerked around when the skid touched the ground on landing. A large bungee helped dampen the shock of landing and taxiing."

Empennage

"The tail surfaces were in excellent condition, with all parts available, and required little more than the usual cleaning, chemical treatment of metal parts, and refinishing. The only unusual feature in the construction was the trailing edge of the rudder and elevator, which was of metal. It attached to the ribs with screws, and was then wrapped in linen."

Wings

"The wings looked like stock items, just out of the factory, when the fabric was peeled back for inspection; there was, however, some delaminated plywood that had to be tended to, and closer inspection revealed that some damage had been done in storage to some of the ribs.

"Some of the false ribs, used to maintain the profile of the airfoil in flight on the lower right wing, were broken and had been repaired rather hastily. These were repaired to production standard. There was also a broken drag wire in the inner bay on the lower right wing.

"There were differences in the construction of the upper and lower wings. The lower wings, near the root, had heavier ribs to support the weight of the wing walk, and the upper wings had had additional ribs inserted in the area covered by prop wash, to prevent fabric flutter. Curiously, although the wings are fitted with navigation lights and a flare dispenser, no electrical wiring was provided to these items. It was evidently just an afterthought applied at the factory prior to delivery to the Smithsonian.

"Like the fuselage vertical and horizontal members, the wing struts are not actually fastened to the wings, but are held in sockets by the interplane cables."

Finishing

"The surfaces were covered with Irish linen, of a very coarse weave. The fabric was first sewn into panels, then laid on the surfaces and dope lapped around all the edges. Reinforced tape, one inch wide on the smaller ribs, two inches wide on the larger was then applied, with stitching every four inches. Over the stitching, a 2¼″ tape was applied, with each edge frayed approximately ¼″—about *one mile* of tape was used on the plane.

"The fabric received six coats of butyrate, non-tautening dope, natural color. The fuselage received a base coat of silver on its lower surfaces; the entire fuselage was then painted cream with a hand brush. The brown paint on the top was sprayed on.

"The original misplaced star insignia were applied again, as were the tail markings, which were not only reversed, but featured a much darker blue than was standard."

Odds and Ends

"The four guns—two Lewis and two Marlin—were stripped, chemically treated, reblued and reassembled. The firing pins were reinstalled, but altered so that they were no longer functional. The Wimperis bombsight was really quite sophisticated, having four adjustments to be used for horizontal and vertical, for wind drift and for sighting. It is made up primarily of brass, with some black painted steel components.

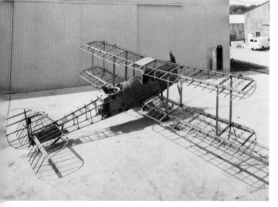

The assembled aircraft is photographed prior to covering. Good details for the master model builder.

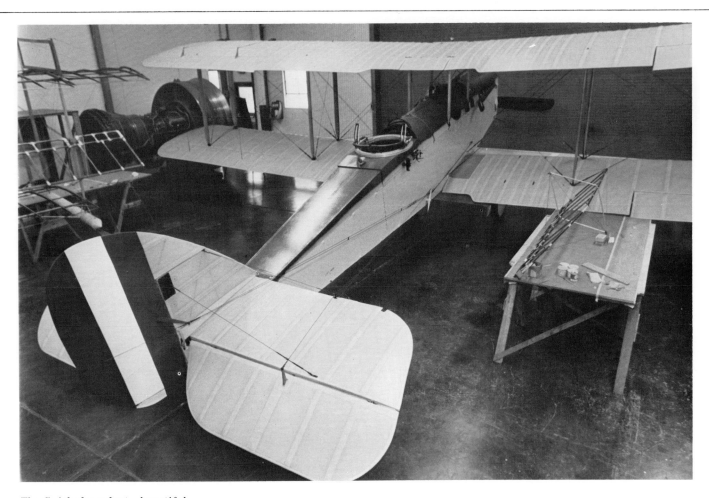

The finished product—beautiful covering job.

Empennage details.

"The wheels had originally been painted the same green color used on the fuel tank, camera, and center section fuel tank. They were highlighted with very elaborate wheel caps with a grease fitting built in. The cap is a bronze casting with the words "Dayton Wright" and a set of wings with an American insignia portrayed on it. Only one was available, and Bill Stevens cast one in brass, not having a bronze casting capability. The wheels thus have two similar castings, differing only in the color of the metal."

Roll Out

"The airplane was completed and rolled out on November 13, 1981, for an intensive photographic session. A total of 4,163 man hours went into the aircraft restoration, of which 3,845 were direct restoration work, and the remaining were programming, photos, etc. Total manhour cost was $40,842.89, while materials cost $3,261.49. Thus for an inexpensive $44,104.38, the United States now has a perfect example of a de Havilland DH-4, built by Dayton-Wright, now perhaps the most tangible artifact of the $640,000,000 appropriation that amazed the world in 1917.

What a beautiful job on a beautiful airplane. Note how star insignia is skewed on undersurface of the wing.

	1917 Rumpler CV[1]	D.H.4[2]	D.H.4[2]	DH-4[2]
Engine	Mercedes D IV a	Rolls-Royce Eagle Mk III	Rolls-Royce Eagle VIII	Liberty 12
Horsepower	260	250	375	400
Speed mph	105.6 @ sea level 100.6 @ 9842' 86.9 @ 16404'	— 113 @ 10000' 102.5 @ 15000'	143 @ sea level 136.5 @ 9000' 122.5 @ 16000"	124.7 @ sea level 117 @ 10000' 113 @ 15000'
Service Ceiling	22309'	16000'	22000'	19500'
Range	364 mi.	3½ hrs.	3¾ hrs.	3 hrs.
Bomb Load	220 lb.	460 lb.	460 lb.	322 lb.
Span	41.53'	42' 4⅝"	42' 4⅝"	42' 5¾"
Length	26.9'	30'8"	30'8"	30' 5⁶¹⁄₆₄"
Height	10.5'	10.5'	11'	10' 3²⁰⁄₃₂"
Wing Area	374.4 sq.ft.	434 sq.ft.	434 sq.ft.	434 sq.ft.
Wing Loading	11.6 lb./sq.ft.	7.6 lb./sq.ft.	8 lb./sq.ft.	9.9 lb./sq.ft.
Power Loading	16.7 lb./HP	13.3 lb./HP	9.3 lb./HP	10.7 lb./HP
Crew Weight	353 lb.	360 lb.	360 lb.	360 lb.
Useful Load	1792 lb.[3]	650 lb.	724 lb.	1546 lb.
Gross Weight	4334 lb.	3313 lb.	3472 lb.	4297 lb.
Crew	2	2	2	2
Armament	1 fixed 7.9mm MG, 1 free-firing 7.9mm MG	1 fixed .303 cal MG, 1 free-firing .303 cal MG	1 fixed .303 cal MG, 1 free firing .303 cal MG	2 fixed .30 cal MG 2 free-firing .30 cal MG

[1] Günter Kroschel and Helmut Strützer, *Die deutschen Militärflugzeuge 1910-1918*, Hereford, West Germany: E.S. Mittler & Sohn, GMBTT, 1977, p. 147.

[2] J.M. Bruce, *British Aeroplanes 1914-1918*, London: Putnam, 1957, pp. 178-180.

[3] Includes weight of crew.

(*Courtesy Robert L. Cavanagh*)

OBSERVATION PLANES—PERFORMANCE COMPARISONS

Summary

The following table summarizes the performance data for all models listed. The order of arrangement is based on speed. Any judgment as to the relative merits of different models based on speed alone, however, is likely to be erroneous, as high speed, while desirable, is but one of the important characteristics in the performance of a successful observation machine. The American De Havilland 4, for example, excels all other models in speed, but has very short endurance. The British De Havilland 4 has both high speed and long endurance, but does not equal the American model in climb and ceiling.

SUMMARY TABLE OF PERFORMANCE

	HP	Speed (Miles)	Climb (Min. Sec.)		Ceiling (Feet)	Endurance (Hrs. Min.)	
American							
De Havilland 4	400	118	7	12	19,700	1	53
French							
Salmson 2A2.	270	116	7	15	20,300	2	45
Spad 16A2.	250	115	7	00	21,300	1	45
Breguet 14A2.	310	114	7	40	21,300	2	45
Caudron 11A3.	430	112	8	10	19,400	3	00
British							
De Havilland 4	240	117.5	11	00	17,500	4	30
De Havilland 9	240	116.9	9	18	17,500	4	30
Bristol Fighter	200	108	8	06	17,000	4	00
R.E. 8	160	98	21	00	13,000	3	30
Italian							
Pomilio E.	290	117	9	30	23,000	3	15
S.I.A. 7Ba.	290	106	13	00	26,200	3	30
S.A.M.L.	260	97	11	15	19,700	3	00

SUMMARY - OBSERVATION

BOMBING PLANES—PERFORMANCE COMPARISONS

Summary

The following table summarizes the performance data for all the models listed, classified by country of manufacture. The order of arrangement for night bombers is based on endurance, and for day bombers on bomb-carrying capacity.

NIGHT BOMBERS

	HP	Endurance (Hrs. Min.)	Bomb Load (Pounds)	Speed (Miles)	Ceiling (Feet)	Climb (Min. Sec.)
British						
Handley Page	600	9 30	1,790	80	8,000	33 18
F.E. 2B	160	3 30	330	81	11,000	18 54
Italian						
Caproni 4	870	5 30	3,300	75	13,000	26 00
Caproni 5	870	5 00	1,760	95	19,000	16 00
Caproni 3	540	4 15	880	84	18,000	16 00
French						
Caproni Bn3.	540	6 00	880	84	16,400	23 50
Voisin 8Bn2.	220	4 00	220	75	14,100	17 20

DAY BOMBERS

	HP	Endurance (Hrs. Min.)	Bomb Load (Pounds)	Speed (Miles)	Ceiling (Feet)	Climb (Min. Sec.)
Italian						
S.I.A. 9B.	685	3 00	770	129	23,000	8 00
Caproni 5	870	5 00	660	96.3	21,300	13 33
French						
Breguet 14B2.	300	2 45	520	110	19,000	9 15
British						
De Havilland 9	240	4 30	380	113.6	15,500	11 24
De Havilland 4	240	4 30	370	108	13,500	13 06
American						
De Havilland 4	400	1 48	220	112	15,000	8 36

SUMMARY - BOMBING

WEIGHTS—DeH-4

Dayton-Wright Machine	
First Built Water And Oil	2404 lbs.
Gas	461 "
Pilot And Passenger	341 "

WEIGHTS—MILITARY LOAD

Bombs (Release Included)	288 lbs. (half (5) under each wing)
Wireless Telephone	60 lbs.
Synchroniser Guns, one 57¼ lbs., two	88¼ lbs.
Flexible Guns, One, (magazine included)	123 lbs.
Camera	54 lbs.
Oxygen Tanks	26 lbs.
	639¼ lbs.

Complete total . . . . 3845¼ lbs.

CLIMB

5000 ft. - 3' 20"   (without full military load)
10000 ft. - 7' 42"

Mr. R.R. Grant   April 22, 1918.

1. Pursuant to instructions the following schedule has been prepared on the DeHavilland 4.

2. On April 16th, 1918, DeHavilland 4 Airplane No. 30. Dayton Wright Series was weighed at South Field, Ohio, showing a total weight of 3737 lbs. with all equipment aboard but no pilot or gunner.

3. On April 20th, 1918, a DeHavilland 4 Airplane was weighed at South Field, Ohio, showing a bare weight of 2337 lbs.

4. The weight equipped as a fighter is as follows:

Bare Plane	2337 lbs.
Oxygen Apparatus	23
2 Marlin guns and 1000 rounds	122
Synchroniser	35
2 Lewis guns and 1000 rounds	128
Aldis sight	5
Ring and bead sights	4
Jumellage	4
2 Fire Extinguishers	13
Instruments	20
Scarff mount	23
Water	126
Gasoline	461
Oil	25
Total wt. without pilot and gunner	3326 lbs.

5.   The weight equipped as a Reconnaissance plane is as follows:

Bare plane	2337
Radio complete	50
Camera complete	50
2 Marlin guns and 1000 rounds	122
Synchroniser	35
2 Lewis guns and 1000 rounds	128
Aldis sight	5
Ring and bead sights	4
Jumellage	4
Heating and lighting apparatus	38
2 Fire extinguishers	13
Instruments	20
Scarff mount	23
Water	124
Gasoline	461
Oil	25
Total weight without pilot and observer.	3439 lbs.

6.   The weight equipped as a bombing plane is as follows:

Bare plane	2337
Radio	50
2 Marlin guns and 1000 rounds	122
Synchroniser	35
2 Lewis guns and 1000 rounds	128
Bombing Apparatus	310
Aldis sight	5
Ring and bead sights	4
Jumellage	4
Wimperis bombing sight	3
Heating and lighting apparatus	38
2 Fire extinguishers	13
Holt flare	5
Very pistol	7
Instruments	20
Scarff mount	126
Gasoline	461
Oil	25
Total weight without pilot and gunner	3693 lbs.

S.J. Twining
A.M.E.

Weights taken at Dayton Wright Co.

Aug. 3, 1918.

By C.E. Booth

Item	Weight	Remarks
Mayo Radiator	97 lbs.	Empty
Gasoline Tank	47	66 gal. tank empty
Lewis gun	18 lbs. 6 ozs.	
Lewis gun magazine	2 6	
97 rounds ammunition		
for Lewis gun	5 5	
100 rounds ammunition		
for Marlin gun	6 7	
Weight of DH-4 Machine, light, without oil, gas, water, men - 2320 lbs.		
Weight of DH-4 Machine, heavy -		3700 lbs.

DH-4 Veneer Cowling:

Pilot's front cowl	21½ lbs.	
Gas Tank	2½	
Rear Cowl, complete	25	
Aft Deck	7	
Front Brace	4	
Wheel and tire	22	
Tail skid and rubber	7	
Bare fuselage, less seats	257	
Pilot seat and cushion	6½	
Passenger seat	2	
Passenger's floor assy.	21	
Pilot's floor assy.	23	
Radiator cowling	5	
Hinges, etc.	2½	
Pass. seat	5	
Instruments:	10	

Watch	motometer
2 aneroids	compass
oil gauge	2 air speed
air gauge	Tachometer & shaft

DH-4 Original

WEIGHT OF FUSELAGE, WITH PARTS LISTED BELOW INCLUDED
WITHIN 340 lbs. 11 0zs.

Longerons
Struts vertical
Braces
Veneers, sides both front and rear fuselage
Veneer bottoms
Linen on rear fuselage
Wires and tie rods
Packing blocks
Front cowling
Rear cowling
Instrument board
Cross struts
Flooring
Pilot's rudder bar support
Pass. rudder bar support
Motor bearers and supports
Wood parts for front gun mount
Camera bracket
Telephone bracket
Cowling over and under motor
Screws, tacks, bolts, linen, tape, cotters, washers, and
   fittings used to make up fuselage

DeH-4 Weights DWA M/C

April 6, 1918.

Weight of main planes:
  Covered and doped, complete with fittings
  (internal bracing wires and internal fitting)
  Aileron pulleys, fork bolts for struts, wing
  skids, external wiring plates, etc.

2 upper - each	77 lbs.
2 lower - each	86¼ lbs.

Weight of ailerons:
  Covered and doped, complete with levers, hinges, etc. — 16 lbs.

Weight of center plane:
  Covered and doped, complete including gravity tank — 40½
  Complete without gravity tank — 20

Stabilizer:
  Covered and doped, complete with fittings, internal wiring plates: — 28½
    Complete with control cables, pulleys, and brace wires — 33½

Elevator:
  Covered and doped, complete with hinges, bolts, levers, etc. each — 8½

Fin:
  Covered and doped, complete with fittings — 6¾

Rudder:
  Covered and doped, complete with fittings — 11½

Fuselage (without engine):
  Front part including controls, sets, cowling, etc.
  Rear part - including fabric, tail skid and tail plane elevating gear

Under-carriage:
  Complete with wheels, tires, covers, axle fairings, bracing wires
  and fittings — 129 lbs.

Struts:
  Twelve interplane struts complete with fittings, including
  Venturi Tubing — 58¼

Radiator:
  Livingston Radiator for Liberty Motor — 112 lbs.

WEIGHTS OF WINGS, etc.
TAKEN AT DAYTON-WRIGHT AIRPLANE CO.

By C.E. Booth

3–28–18

Item	Not Covered	Covered
Right wing, upper	62 lb.	77 lbs.
Right wing, lower	64.5	76
Right aileron, upper	12	15
Right aileron, lower	12	15
Center section	31.5	39
Stabilizer	21	25.5
Right Elevator	7	8.5
Left Elevator	7	8.5
Fin	4.5	5.5
Rudder	9	11.5
	230.5	281.5
Difference		230.5
		51.0

Right side rear fuselage canvas not on. This can be neglected.

WEIGHTS OF PARTS AND INSTRUMENTS
USED ON SAMPLE SHIP

Interphone box including batteries and hinges	5 lbs.	1 oz.
Operating cam for bomb dropping device in bottom of fuselage	4 lbs.	4 oz.
Cartridge	395 Gr.	
Generator brackets for generators on landing gear struts	3 lbs.	8 oz.
Tail lamp on rear cowling		14 oz.
Helmet complete with telephone set	2½ lbs.	
Lamp bracket used on end of wing for holt flare light	1 lb.	
Oxygen tank	30 lbs.	
Bomb	23 lbs.	
Nose for propellor hub		8½ oz.
Bolt		1½ oz.
3 ply ring		1 oz.
Battery box for battery in pilot's cockpit	1 lb.	7 oz.
Willard Storage Battery (Type S-Y-P-13)	10 lbs.	
1 qt. Pyrene fire extinguisher (Pump type No. 154678)	5 lb.	7 oz.
Pargon propellor for generator		15 oz.
Pargon propellor for generator	1 lb.	3¾ oz.
Bomb dropping sight	4 lb.	8 oz.
Generator on left hand strut of landing gear	17 lb.	3 oz.
Bomb dropping device under wing	25 lb.	3 oz.
Bomb dropping release handle	2 lb.	3 oz.
Camera operating lever	1 lb.	6 oz.
Emergency battery box	2 lb.	10 oz.
Sperry gyroscope	5 lb.	6 oz.
Filter for wireless set	5 lb.	6 oz.
U.S. Aero reel	5 lb.	6 oz.
Signal Corps U.S. Army aeroplane radio transmitting and receiving set	18 lb.	11 oz.
Signal Corps U.S.A. two passenger's oxygen apparatus	3 lb.	14 oz.
U.S. Fairlead		10 ozs.

WAR DEPARTMENT
Office of the Chief of Air Service
Washington

01–5–15
2 Pages
Pages 1

March 16, 1925.

Technical Order
No. 01–5–15

AIRPLANES AND PARTS
DH-4 Type - Symbols for Special Airplanes

1. The following are authorized symbols for use of DH-4 type airplanes. Hereafter all airplanes of this type will be known and reported by these symbols. The characteristics of planes of the type which cover their symbol designation will not be changed without prior authority from the Chief Air Service or the Field Service Section.

DH-4B	Standard Liberty 12 installation—88 gallon, plain, main gas tank—96 gallon total fuel capacity
DH-4B1	Standard Liberty 12 installation—110 gallon main gas tank—118 gallon total fuel capacity
DH-4B2	Standard Liberty 12 installation—76 gallon, leak-proof main gas tank—83 gallon total fuel capacity
DH-4B3	Standard Liberty 12 installation—135 gallon main gas tank—143 gallon total fuel capacity
DH-4B4	Airways airplane with Liberty 12 installation prepared in accordance with drawing No. 0104000—110 gallon main gas tank—118 gallon fuel capacity
DH-4BD	Duster airplane, standard DH-4B equipped with duster apparatus
DH-4BG	Gas Barrage airplane, standard DH-4B equipped with smoke screen apparatus
DH-4BM	Standard DH-4B airplane modified with rear seat and rear baggage compartment only
DH-4BM1	Transport type airplane, built in accordance with specifications from Office, Chief of Air Service—dual control, including instruments—110 gallon main gas tank—118 gallon total fuel capacity
DH-4BM2	Transport type airplane, built in accordance with specifications from Office, Chief of Air Service—135 gallon main gas tank—143 gallon total fuel capacity
DH-4BK	Standard DH-4B airplane equipped for night flying
DH-4BP1	Photographic airplane, Liberty 12 installation, adapted to vertical mapping, oblique and motion picture photography in accordance with drawing No. X-39241
DH-4BP3	Photographic airplane, Liberty 12 installation, adapted to vertical mapping, oblique and motion picture photography in accordance with drawing No. X-47746, 110 gallon main gasoline tank—118 gallon total fuel capacity
DH-4BT	Training airplane, standard DH-4B modified air dual control including instruments and rear seat
DH-4M1	Liberty 12 installation, metal fuselage in accordance with A.S. Specification 1560 or A.S. Specification 1561-B—76 gallon main gas tank—83 gallon total fuel capacity
DH-4M2	Liberty 12 installation, metal fuselage in accordance with A.S. Specification 1567—110 gallon main gas tank—118 gallon total fuel capacity
DH-4M2P	Photographic airplane, Liberty 12 installation, metal fuselage in accordance with A.S. Specification 1569—110 gallon main gas tank—118 gallon total fuel capacity
DH-4M2S	Supercharger airplane, Liberty 12 installation, metal fuselage in accordance with A.S. Specification 1568—88 gallon main gas tank—96 gallon total fuel capacity
XDH-4BP	Experimental photographic airplane, Liberty 12 installation—cameras mounted in front cockpit
XDH-4BP2	Experimental photographic airplane, Liberty 12 installation—135 gallon main gas tank—96 gallon total fuel capacity USD-9A wings
XDH-4BS	Experimental airplane, Liberty 12 engine equipped with supercharger in accordance with drawing No. X-38250—88 gallon main gas tank—96 gallon total fuel capacity

XDH-4L Experimental airplane, Liberty 12 installation, 185 gallon main gas tank, 9 hour plane

XDH-4B5 Experimental airways airplane built in accordance with Engineering Division's drawings for carrying passengers or freight.

By order of the Chief of Air Service.

W.G. Kilner,
Major, Air Service
Executive

This Technical Order replaces Technical Order 01-5-15 dated May 5, 1924.

V-4763, A.S., Rev 3/16/25.

01–5–15
2 Pages
Page 2

V-4763, A.S., Rev 3/16/25.

AMERICAN EXPEDITIONARY FORCES
HEADQUARTERS AIR PRODUCTION CENTER NO. 2
FRANCE.

August 22, 1918

PROCEEDINGS OF A BOARD OF OFFICERS DELEGATED TO PASS ON
SUGGESTED CHANGES IN LIBERTY ENGINE AND DH-4 AIRPLANE.

Pursuant to verbal instructions from Colonel Dunwoody, Air Service Hdqrs. Paris, a Board of Officers met on August 22, 23, and 24, 1918, at Romorantin, France, for the purpose of passing on suggested changes in Liberty Motor and DH-4 Airplane: Present:

Lieut. Col. Hall,	Major Riley
Lieut. Col. Harms,	Major Wardwell,
Major Bell,	Capt. Marsh,
Major Marmon,	Lieut. Stahl (Navy)

Major Wardwell acted as Chairman.

PROPELLERS

1. Col. Hall reports that arrangements have been made for rectifying the errors in propellers and shortly those coming from the States will not show the defects prevalent in the others.

2. *PROPELLER HUB SHIMS:* Instructions to be given to the Propeller Department that all hubs shall be brought to a standard thickness so that a uniform length of propeller hub belt can be used.

RADIATORS

1. *Radiator Supports:* Col. Hall reports that radiator has been equipped with a strip catching hold of the core in the inside, transferring the weight directly to the bracket, which will obviate further trouble from leaks in this location. The committee considers that there is no general action to be taken to overcome the difficulty in the radiators which have already been shipped.

2. Col. Hall reports that hereafter all planes will have long type radiators, and that shutters designed to cover the entire surface are being put into production. For planes now in service the squadrons will be advised to blanket whatever portion of the radiating surface is necessary.

The U.S. will be requested to leave off the radiator cowling as soon as practicable and to round off the edges of the radiator.

The holes in the upper radiator brackets should be $\frac{1}{16}''$ larger than the bolts. The U.S. will be requested to make this change.

The Malivert check valve and bottom filler for radiator has been ordered by the Supply Section and an adapting nipple will be made for screwing into the pipe. These when ready will be fitted to all planes, and samples will be sent to the U.S. with request that it be supplied in the future. It is estimated that a stock of a 1000 will be required before the arrival of the connections from the States.

FUSELAGE

1. *ALTITUDE CONTROL:* It is recommended that the U.S. be instructed to put into production immediately on all planes, the type of articulated altitude carburetor control, same as that now being incorporated on planes being built by the Standard Aero Corporation.

2. *INTERPLANE STRUT FITTING:* U.S. is to be instructed to lengthen the fitting in the upper ends of the interplane struts so as to permit the clevis pins connecting the flying and landing wires in the outer panel to be put in head up. The Technical Section to make up suitable drawings and send the necessary instructions to the U.S.

3. *PILOT'S SEAT:* U.S. to be instructed to raise the pilot's seat three inches, using present method of construction. For planes fitted with the tank under the pilot's seat, the construction will be as necessary.

4. *JOY STICK:* Technical Section will design and substitute a non-magnetic joy stick to be placed in those machines now here and those coming from the U.S.

5. *FRONT DOOR SPRINGS:* Instructions will be sent to the U.S. requesting an increase in the strength of the springs on the front door hinges.

6. *CLEARANCE - CENTER SECTION STRUTS:* U.S. will be requested to provide ¼″ clearance between the center section strut and the cowling.

7. *DRIFT WIRE ANCHORAGE:* It is recommended that the three belts attaching the forward drift wires to the front end of the lower longeron be removed, putting in their place two ¼″ rods extending across the front of the machine with castellated nuts and cotters on each end and lock nuts and washers on the inside of each longeron. Col. Hall reports that the machines now coming from the U.S. will be so equipped.

8. *RUDDER BAR STRAPS:* Instructions should be sent to the U.S. to equip the rudder bar in the pilot's cockpit with straps for holding the feet to the rudder bar.

9. *COVERS:* The U.S should be instructed to supply covers for the forward and after cockpit on each machine with ¼″ cotton ropes of sufficient length to tie under the fuselage. If possible the two covers should also be made of the same pattern. Propeller covers should also be provided and one supplied with each machine. These should be made of some dark material. 1,000 extra sets should be furnished for the machines already shipped and to make up losses. They should be suitably waterproofed and of duck or other material. The States should be instructed to cancel any outstanding orders for long fuselage covers now being made.

10. *RADIATOR COWLING COVER:* The U.S. will be instructed to furnish 1,000 radiator cowling blanket covers. Design and sample to be furnished by Technical Section and furnished to the U.S.

11. *CENTER SECTION STRUT SUPPORT:* U.S. should be instructed to change support to front center section struts on top of longeron to conform to design of English fitting. Design to be furnished by the Technical Section.

12. *AIR PUMP HANDLE:* U.S. should be instructed to arrange device for holding air pump handle down free from gas control. Sufficient quantity should be sent from the U.S. to equip planes already shipped.

13. *FASTENING OF SPARE JOY STICK:* U.S. to be instructed to substitute a small strop for the spring clip now arranged for holding the spare joy stick in the observers cockpit.

14. *INTERPLANE OR CENTER SECTION STRUTS:* U.S. to be instructed that no poplar interplane or center section struts be used.

15. *AUXILIARY RUDDER-CONTROL:* It is recommended that the U.S. be instructed to put into production as soon as possible, auxiliary rudder control according to the plans and specifications supplied by the Technical Section, and duplicate set now being furnished by Capt. Marsh to Col. Hall.

RIGGING, WIRES & CABLES

1. *WRAPPING CABLES:* Col. Hall reports that the U.S. is now using sperm candles for soldering flux, doing away with the difficulty that has been experienced with the wrapping of wires.

2. *FAIRING ON FLYING WIRES:* Based upon report of Col. Hall of experience in the U.S. which shows that there is no advantage in speed for having the fairing on flying wires, it is recommended that this be omitted on planes assembled hereafter. The points in favor of the omission of this fairing are that it makes inspection easier, does not provide means of covering up injury done to the wires, and also makes it easier to re-rig the airplane.

3. *AILERON CONTROL WIRE GUIDES:* Col. Hall reports that the aileron control wires are now being guided through rawhide bushings to prevent fraying where they pass through and along the edge of the plane.

4. *AILERON COMPENSATING WIRES:* U.S. to be instructed to provide the barrels of the turnbuckles ¼″ longer so as to permit additional adjustment.

5. *AILERON PULLEY BOLT:* U.S. to be instructed to place fillet under the head of the aileron pulley belt, and that same should be softer. A number of them have failed in service due to being too hard.

EMPENNAGE

1. *TAIL SKID POST:* It is recommended that the U.S. be instructed to reinforce the tail skid post for a length of 6 inches from its lower end by insertion of a steel tube of approximately 16 gauge.

2. *REINFORCEMENT OF WING SURFACES:* Col. Hall reports that the U.S. is now reinforcing both the lower wings by the addition of extra ribs between the existing ribs so as to protect against the action of the slip stream of the propeller. It is recommended that planes now here be reinforced in the same place by tacking thin strips of spruce above and below the wings over the ribs on each lower wing between the fuselage and the inner struts, similar to the Caproni.

UNDERCARRIAGE

1. *SHOCK ABSORBERS:* It is recommended that the U.S be instructed to furnish suitable shock absorber rubber like samples furnished by Technical Section. Captain Marsh reported having already sent to the U.S. samples of properly wound shock absorber rubber, and is to furnish Col. Hall with samples and specifications so that this may be properly followed up.

The Technical Section will furnish elongation curves made up from examination of various shock absorbers now in use in France, so as to provide for uniform results being obtained with various types of shock.

2. *STRUT REINFORCEMENT:* Col. Hall reports that the U.S. is reinforcing the saddles over which the shock absorber is wound and increasing the length of same by ½″ at each end to provide for the proper number of turns, and that meanwhile, there is nothing that can be done to correct the present fault.

3. *AXLES:* It is recommended that the U.S. be instructed to fit all axles with 14″ ash fillers in each and centered under saddles. The fillers to be made in two halves, with 4 m/m steel strip in the center running full length. The filler to be a snug fit and placed with the steel reinforcement vertical to landing position.

4. *HUB GAP:* Col. Hall reports that the axle caps now being furnished from the U.S. will be fitted with bolts and castellated nuts with cotter pins, in place of the taper pin now used. It is recommended that provision be made at once to make this change on all planes now delivered.

5. *STRUT BRACKETS:* Recommend that the U.S. be instructed to make landing gear strut brackets which shall attach to lower longeron in one piece.

TAIL SKIDS

1. The U.S. to be instructed to furnish tail skids in accordance with design and specifications to be furnished by Technical Section. The rubber for this skid is to be ½″ wide, 8 ft. 8″ long, with 6 turns and 4½″ lap in the wrapping. Col. Hall reports that the tail skids are now being furnished by the U.S. equipped with steel shoes, and that extra shoes are coming from the U.S. for planes already shipped. Meanwhile, special cast shoes are being obtained locally to fill immediate requirements, and Romorantin will continue to reinforce tail skid as at present.

PHOTOGRAPHIC EQUIPMENT

1. Col. Hall and Capt. Marsh will have conference with Photographic Section in Paris with a view to specifying the proper equipment.

RADIO AND TELEPHONES

1. Col. Hall reports that planes now coming from the U.S. are arranged to take any and all the equipment being furnished from the U.S., together with such brackets and fittings as are necessary.

INSTRUMENTS

1. *AIR SPEED INDICATORS:* It is reported that American DH 4's are now being received with the Ogilvie Air Speed Indicator and that in view of the fact that other types are being put into production in the U.S., it is recommended that immediate experiments be made to determine which type will be most successful. And that the Technical Section undertake to send the necessary instructions to the U.S.

IGNITION

1. *DELCO SYSTEM:* It is recommended that the U.S. be instructed to provide an enclosed battery box so as to protect the battery against mechanical injury or short circuit. Request that more careful provision be made to protect against oil entering the distributor head. Also that attention of the U.S. be called to the necessity for a more careful inspection of the Delco system.

2. *ELECTRIC VIBRATING STARTING COIL:* It is recommended that the U.S be instructed to equip all planes with electric vibrating starting coil, 1,000 extra sets to be supplied

immediately and used for equipping planes already shipped from the U.S., and that 10% extra spares be supplies to cover subsequent shipments.

ARMAMENT

1. *TOURELLE:* It is recommended that the U.S. be instructed to cancel tourelles that are in production and to endeavor to rebuild these in accordance with the French standard, sample of which and drawings are being supplied by the Armament Department. The desired design is the French tourelle T-O 3.

2. *OBSERVER'S COCKPIT:* The Technical Section will supply detailed design for new seat in observer's cockpit and for re-arrangement of instruments and equipment. These to be sent to U.S. with instructions to put into production as soon as possible.

GAS AND OIL TANKS

1. *OIL TANKS:*

(a) All planes received to date have one oil tank of 4½ gallons capacity. Plane now floated and all planes hereafter to be floated will have two such tanks, and this 9 gallon total will be satisfactory, provided the gasoline capacity is not increased to more than 100 gallons. The necessary oil tanks for providing two on all planes now here are expected to arrive soon from the U.S.; but to avoid possible delay, the Supply Section will manufacture tanks and will install them, or will send them to the Squadrons for installation. The two tanks of any one plane will be right and left-hand, and not interchangeable.

(b) Technical Section will design a complete adapter or suitable funnel for the oil tank inlets, to be put into production at Romorantin.

(c) Cable to be sent immediately to the U.S. requesting courier be sent with 100 right hand tanks with complete set of fittings for double tank installation. To be followed by immediate shipment of 400 additional sets. The extra oil tank is of the same design as the present oil tank but it is rolled on the opposite side and installed in the same manner. It is fitted with ⅜″ vents and filler caps. This alteration is being included in all planes coming forward from the States. Tanks may have to be filled from both sides.

2. *GASOLINE TANKS:*

(a) All planes received to date have gasoline capacity of approximately 69 gallons in main tanks and 7 in "nourrice," making 76 total. Planes now believed to be floated and probably already in French ports, and all planes hereafter to be floated, will have same sized nourrice and an 88 gallon main tank, making 95 gallons total. Supply Section now has design for a 24 gallon tank to be located under pilot's seat. Supply Section will manufacture this and install or furnish for all planes now in France, thereby giving such planes a total of 100 gallons.

(b) The desirability of having the largest possible gasoline capacity has been given full consideration by this Committee, but it considered advisable to limit the capacity to 100 gallons on the D.H.4 plane. Larger capacity is provided on the D.H.9 but it requires larger wing surface. 100 gallons of gas should give the D.H.4 fully 500 miles of average flying.

(c) The Technical Section will furnish design for an improved filler plug for the main gas tank, and sample plug with drawings will be sent to the States with request that it be supplied as soon as it can be put into production.

(d) Planes soon to arrive will have the nourrice drained by a tube running back along the surface of the center section. Planes hereafter assembled at Production Center No. 2 will be similarly fitted, and if experience shows that this is necessary, squadrons will be advised to make this change on planes now in service, instead of conducting the drain tube downward along the landing strut.

3. *PROTECTED GAS TANKS:*

Col. Hall reports that the States are attempting to install a satisfactory non-leakable main gas tank. This will reduce the gas capacity of the plane by about 10 gallons, making the capacity about 88 gallons. Technical Section will go into this question with Colonel Hall with a view to making a selection of suitable tank, and decide what recommendation shall be sent to the States in this connection.

ENGINE

1. *CARBURETORS:*

(a) Carburetors on planes assembled at A.P.C. #2 will be fitted with U-shaped air inlet scoops now being made in Paris. These scoops will be drained at both ends. Until these scoops are ready, the use of two scoops bolted together will continue.

(b) Planes hereafter assembled will have their carburetors modified as shown on Technical Section drawing No. 2017, until the arrival of planes with modified carburetors from the States.

Colonel Hall reports that the States are putting into production a carburetor and scoop arrangement modified to conform to the Technical Section drawing No. 2017.

(c) Choke tubes and jets on carburetors hereafter to be received from the U.S. will not be changed unless future experience shows it to be necessary. Carburetors on most of the planes thus far sent out from A.P.C. #2 have had 36 m/m choke tubes. This size is considered to be too large for Packard engines No. 1 to 900 and Lincoln engines No. 1 to 350, because these engines have light crank shafts or light bearings, and their maximum power should be limited by using 31 mm. choke tubes. The choke tubes on planes already sent out need not be changed unless trouble is reported, but when any of the above numbered engines are overhauled, 31 mm. choke and 140 main jets with 150 compensators should be substituted, and at the same time, the heavy type connecting rods and bearings should be put in if possible. Above numbered engines should be overhauled after 25 hours running.

(d) Colonel Hall reports that the States now are putting in production gas filters which are to be installed as part of the motor. Until such time as engines arrive with these filters, the special filters as designed by the Technical Section will be secured and installed on planes now being assembled and in service.

(e) It is decided that it was not necessary to cotter the cylinder hold-down stud nuts and that cable be sent to the States to this effect.

2. *OIL PRESSURE:*

Oil pressure on the pumps is to be limited to 25 to 35 lbs. with engines running at maximum revolutions on the butts. Engines which show pressure above or below this should be corrected.

3. *INSTRUCTION BOOKS:*

United States should be instructed that a Liberty Engine Book be packed with each engine, both in the plane and spare engines, and that the quantity of 1,000 books already asked for extra supply be shipped at once.

4. *ENGINE COWLING:*

The U.S. will be requested to equip the planes with upper cowling from which center hinge pin has been omitted. Cable sent to the States to this effect. It is recommended that on the planes now being assembled that the lower rear corners of the upper cowling be cut off and the the hinge that is now attached to the longeron at this point be raised some 6 to 8 inches, so as to permit the cowling to be more easily removed.

PACKING FOR SHIPMENT

1. *PACKING OF FRONT OF FUSELAGE:*

States should be instructed to exercise great care in the packing of the front fuselage, particularly in the support of the motor as since the installation of a large radiator a number of shipments have been received in which the engine bearers have been loosened.

2. *PACKING AILERON BOXES:*

United States should be instructed to pack the ailerons more securely in the boxes. A few of these have been received with the packing strips and blocks dislocated, due to insecure nailing.

Colonel Hall and Captain Marsh will have conference with the Armament Section relative to the notes on Armament Equipment with a view to making subsequent recommendations.

(Signed) E.J. Hall
Elbert J. Hall, Lieut. Colonel, U.S.A.

(Signed) Wm. H. Wardwell
W.H. Wardwell, Major, U.S.A.

(Signed) J.C. Riley
J.C. Riley, Major, U.S.A.

(Signed) J.F. Bell
J.F. Bell, Major, U.S.A.

(Signed) Robert Marsh, Jr.
Robert Marsh, Jr., Captain, U.S.A.

Notes

[1] The English designation was de Havilland D.H.4; the American designation was de Havilland DH-4.

[2] The term "flaming coffin" derived from the apparent ease with which the DH-4 burned in combat. This has been attributed by some to the engine-driven air pressure fuel system. Yet actual analysis of combat losses does not confirm that the DH-4s burned more readily than other aircraft.

[3] There are many planes whose fame derived from this same sort of availability. The Curtiss P-40, famed for its shark-toothed role in the Flying Tiger group, served on every front throughout World War I even though it was often outclassed by enemy aircraft. It was available. Similarly, Douglas DC-3s soldiered on in service for years after World War II, shouldering aside countless replacement aircraft, simply because they were available and because the incremental advances in performance were not worth the substantial increase in cost of production.

[4] The Germans were constrained by their numerical inferiority and by their generally lower powered engines from developing specialized aircraft. Thus the Rumpler C-V was an excellent aircraft, with a high service ceiling, and was able to function on an individual basis over Allied lines. Yet it did not have the versatility of the DH-4.

[5] Technically SPAD for Société pour les Appareils Deperdussin, later Société pour Aviation et ses Dérivés, but Spad is widely used.

[6] "Boom" Trenchard was the father of the Royal Flying Corps and Royal Air Force. His policy was always to take the offensive, regardless of odds, and to carry the battle to the enemy. The result was a curious combination of extremely high casualties to the English Forces and the establishment of a complete morale ascendency over the Germans. This morale factor extends to this day in the Royal Air Force and was of vital significance during World War II.

[7] See complete listing in Appendix B, T.O. 01-5-15, March 16, 1925.

Bibliography

Bowers, Peter M. *The American D.H.4.* Aircraft Profiles Series, no. 97. Leatherhead, Surrey, England: Profile Publications Ltd., 1966.

Bruce, J.M. *British Aeroplanes 1914–1918.* London: Putman, 1957.

Bruce, J.M. *The de Havilland D.H.4.* Aircraft Profile Series, no. 26. Leatherhead, Surrey, England: Profile Publications Ltd., 1965.

Crowell, Benedict. *America's Munitions 1917–1918.* Washington, D.C.: Government Printing Office, 1919.

Gorrell, Edgar S. *The Measure of America's World War Aeronautical Effort* Burlington, Vermont: Lane Press, Inc., 1941.

Jackson, A.J. *De Havilland Aircraft Since 1915.* London: Putnam, 1962.

Kroschel, Günter, and Helmut Stützer. *Die deutschen Militärflugzeuge 1910–1918.* Herford, West Germany: E.S. Mittler & Sohn, Gmbtt, 1977.

Lewis, Peter. *The British Bomber Since 1914.* London: Putnam, 1974.

Marcosson, Isaac F. *Colonel Deeds: Industrial Builder.* New York: Dodd, Mead & Company, 1948.

Maurer, Maurer, ed. *The U.S. Air Service in World War I.* Vols. I-IV. Washington, D.C.: Office of Air Force History, 1978.

Pearson, Henry Greenleaf. *A Business Man in Uniform: Raynal Cawthorne Bolling.* New York: Duffield & Company, 1923.

Smart, Lawrence. *The Hawks that Guided the Guns.* N.p., 1968.

Sweetser, Arthur. *The American Air Service.* New York: D. Appleton and Company, 1919.

ABOUT THE AUTHOR:

WALTER J. BOYNE is the Director of the National Air and Space Museum. Mr. Boyne joined the Museum in 1974, after retiring as a Colonel from the United States Air Force. During his museum career, Mr. Boyne has served in many different capacities. He was Curator of Aeronautics, Chief of Preservation and Restoration, Executive Officer, Assistant Director, Deputy Director, and Acting Director before assuming his present position. One of his first tasks as a Curator was the supervision of the restoration, movement, assembly, installation, and suspension of the artifacts in the new Museum. A Command Pilot with more than 5,000 hours in a score of different types of airplanes, Mr. Boyne is the author of seven books and more than 200 articles on aviation subjects. He lives with his wife and children in Alexandria, Virginia.